Traditional Witchcraft for the Woods and Forests

A Witch's Guide to the Woodland with
Guided Meditations and Pathworking

Traditional Witchcraft for the Woods and Forests

A Witch's Guide to the Woodland with
Guided Meditations and Pathworking

Mélusine Draco

MOON
BOOKS

Winchester, UK
Washington, USA

First published by Moon Books, 2012
Moon Books is an imprint of John Hunt Publishing Ltd., Laurel House, Station Approach,
Alresford, Hants, SO24 9JH, UK
office1@o-books.net
www.o-books.com

For distributor details and how to order please visit the 'Ordering' section on our website.

Text copyright: Mélusine Draco 2011

ISBN: 978 1 84694 803 9

A CIP catalogue record for this book is available from the British Library.

Design: Stuart Davies

Printed in the UK by CPI Antony Rowe
Printed in the USA by Offset Paperback Mfrs, Inc

We operate a distinctive and ethical publishing philosophy in all
areas of our business, from our global network of authors to
production and worldwide distribution.

CONTENTS

Author Biography

Mélusine Draco originally trained in the magical arts of traditional British Old Craft with Bob and Mériém Clay-Egerton. She has been a magical and spiritual instructor for over 20 years with Arcanum and the Temple of Khem, and writer of numerous popular books including *Liber Agyptius: the Book of Egyptian Magic; The Egyptian Book of Days; The Egyptian Book of Nights; The Thelemic Handbook; The Hollow Tree,* an elementary guide to the Qabalah; *A Witch's Treasury of the Countryside; Root & Branch: British Magical Tree Lore* and *Starchild: a rediscovery of stellar wisdom.* Her highly individualistic teaching methods and writing draws on ancient sources, supported by academic texts and current archaeological findings. She now lives in Ireland near the Galtee Mountains.

Both *Traditional Witchcraft for Fields and Hedgerows* and *Traditional Witchcraft for Woods and Forests* assume a certain degree of magical understanding on the part of the reader with regard to routine divination, spell and Circle casting. For this reason, the text does not include the basic elements of rudimentary witchcraft that can be found in titles similar to *Traditional Witchcraft for Urban Living* and *Traditional Witchcraft for the Seashore.*

For Hilary …
companion of the Wild Wood

Chapter One

The Path to Hunter's Wood

In the early strivings of the mind of primitive man to account for the scheme of creation, the tree took a foremost place, and the sky, with its clouds and luminaries, became likened to an enormous Cosmogonic Tree of which the fruits were the sun, moon and stars.
'The Lore of the Forest', Alexander Porteous

Hunter's Wood does not exist in the 'real' world — or rather, different parts of it exist in different locations. Neither is the practice of wood-Craft restricted to any particular witchcraft or pagan tradition since a wooded landscape is pertinent to every creed and culture since ancient times. For the purpose of visualisation, meditation and pathworking, however, we will be using natural broad-leafed woodland, since the fauna and flora of the forest have always played an important role in traditional witchcraft. Many of the ingredients for a witch's spells and charms come from woodland plants and trees, while the fauna offers unique opportunities for divination and augury. Hunter's Wood can be recreated on the inner planes by using magical techniques, so that even those witches living in urban surroundings can take to the woodland paths whenever they choose ... and perhaps come to understand more about traditional wood-Craft and country ways.

First and foremost, forests and woodland have played a mystical role in all cultures where trees have dominated the landscape. Trees bring Nature right up close and personal and, as a result, the whole of the natural world becomes a 'tangled web of enchantment' to a true witch's eyes. Most of us are familiar with what we call 'broad leaved' woodland ... that is to say, forest made up predominantly of trees whose leaves are basically flat, as opposed to being needle-shaped like those of the conifers of the evergreen world. These trees are mostly deciduous (with the exception of the holly, box and strawberry tree), and shed their leaves when winter approaches, lying dormant until the warmth of spring stimulates new growth.

The trees in Hunter's Wood are natives and form part of the great broad-leaved forest that once stretched over the whole of northern Europe. Nevertheless, not all remaining woodland is ancient; nor are all woods that are not ancient, man-made. Left alone, Nature has a tendency to re-colonise almost any land that is allowed to remain idle. Trees such as sycamore, birch and oak, which readily colonise new territory, quickly invade open land and very often relatively new, dense woodland can be found only an hour's drive from the city centre.

In the beginning … Britain's original trees disappeared during the last Ice Age, 10,000 years ago, but by the time the land had separated from continental Europe some 2000 year later, 35 species had returned by natural means — brought in by the wind and birds — as the climate gradually grew warmer. Until man began clearing the forests 5000 years ago, the natural vegetation of much of the British Isles was a blanket of broad-leaved deciduous trees — alder, birch, oak and lime. The myths and legends that grew out of this forest haunted his imagination.

Before we begin to practice the Craft of the wood-witch, however, we must learn to look at trees with different eyes, because there is still a sense of mystery and enchantment in the woodland world. Each month of the year imprints its own beauty on the trees, and in time, we will become aware of every subtle nuance as part of this sacred mantra, with each month bringing different plants for a witch to use in her magical workings. The spring shimmer of birch and beech bursting into life … the cool of a summer glade filled with the whispering of the leaf canopy

... the rich hues of autumn ... branches glistening with hoare frost in the winter sunshine

For the traditional witch, a moment's contemplation becomes an act of homage, just as Japan's indigenous Shinto belief expresses the ritual act of worship in the silent appreciation of the cherry blossom ... or moonlight on a snow-covered garden. This simple poem from Bunya No Asayasu (c. AD 900) was written at the request of the Emperor during a garden party, but it can still conjure up for us a wider mental image of glistening dew drops, sparkling in the morning sunlight ...

In a gust of wind the white dew
On the Autumn grass
Scatters like a broken necklace.

In a similar way, Native Americans also regard the landscape as a living, breathing thing with which they interact as a natural part of their very existence. Take this example from the last words of the great hunter and warrior, Crowfoot, of the Blackfoot Confederacy (1890) ...

What is life? It is the flash of a firefly in the night.
It is the breath of a buffalo in the winter time.
It is the little shadow, which runs across the grass
and loses itself in the Sunset.

These simple but evocative thoughts paint a much larger picture of the wisdom reflected in beliefs deeply rooted in Nature and ancestor worship, and which are possibly the closest to the idealised paganism of modern thinking.

Unfortunately, much of contemporary witchcraft has become bogged down in observing the ritualised rigmarole of calendars and festivals on pre-set days of the year, without ever referring to Nature's unmistakeable way of telling us when the seasonal changes occur, and when there is cause for celebration. What is also hard to understand is the modern trend for many pagan practices to ignore native trees and include introduced species into their tree-lore, despite professing to be following the traditions of indigenous witchcraft. This is, of course, understandable in the case of the wild strawberry tree, for example, which can now only be found growing naturally in Ireland — but where is the alder and the elm, and where is the beech? Why is ellen-wood often listed among the nine sacred woods suitable for the Need-fire, when any seasoned country person would tell you that it can never be burned without some risk to hearth or home?

For our hunter-gatherer ancestors the forest was viewed with a large degree of fear, tempered with mystery; intensified by the deep shadows that lay hidden within its depths, and peopled with hosts of strange beings endowed with superhuman powers. By the Middle Ages much of this primitive woodland had been cleared for agriculture, or large tracts of it enclosed for royal hunting forests, but the Romances of the time still contained many allusions to these mythological and enchanted places so full of magic and witchcraft.

The forest *is* still full of that Romance, where mysterious voices echo in shadowy glades and filmy apparitions glide on the periphery of our vision. Consequently, forests throughout the world have become 'theatres of superstition'; while around many of the trees, legend has spread its imaginary lore.

There *is* still an eerie feeling that we are not alone in this 'theatre' of mysterious ancestral things ... that these things are not merely hidden, but are specially hidden from *us*. Then there comes the sensation that from behind gnarled tree trunks watching eyes are following our every step. A feeling that intensifies as the sun sinks and the light fades ...

The Ancestors
But exactly *who* are these Ancestors that play such an integral

4

part of traditional witchcraft? *Why* is it so important to pay homage to their memory? *What* part do they play? *Where* do they come from? *When* and *how* do we connect with them?

Interaction with them as an invisible and powerful presence, is a constant feature of traditional witchcraft, with the Ancestors remaining important members of the tradition (or people they have left behind), but with additional mystical and/or magical powers. Sometimes they are identified as the Old Ones, who gave magical knowledge to mankind. Or, even more ambiguously 'those who have gone before' — their magical essence distilled into the universal subconscious at different levels. Once contact has been established, the Ancestors can be relied upon to have the interests of the 'tradition' — and therefore the witch's interests — as their primary concern. The Ancestors protect the living, but insist on the maintenance of various customs, and any serious breach of etiquette could result in the removal of their favour.

Reverence for Craft ancestors is part of the ethic of respect for those who have preceded us in life, and their continued presence on the periphery of our consciousness means that they are always with us. And because traditional witchcraft is essentially a practical thing, the Ancestors are called upon to help find solutions to magical problems through divination, path-working and spell-casting. Although witchcraft is *not* a religion, the belief in the ancestral spirits goes hand in hand with a deep reverence for Nature and the Wild Wood.

Exploring Hunter's Wood

Hunter's Wood, however, is a dreamscape that a witch can visit at any time, should we feel the need to harness the timeless energy of the Wild Wood, regardless of time or season. For visualisation purposes, the Wood is approximately ten acres in size, flanked by a fast running stream to the east and a long ride, or track, to the west. A ride is a treeless break in forested areas used in ancient times for the hunting of deer — hence the name of this wood. The stream feeds a woodland pool with a slow trickle during the summer months, but when the winter rains come all the accumulated dead leaves and twigs will be swept away by the torrent. The southern edge of the wood opens onto a huge cornfield, in the centre of which is a large mound, crowned by a stand of three Scots pines; while to the north there is a wide expanse of marshy heathland with its alder carr. Narrow paths criss-cross the wood: some are old and man-made, others are animal tracks, but all will lead us deeper into the woodland realm.

This Wood is *old*. It has grown old alongside humanity and bears the evidence of its passing; generations of witches have wandered in secret glades, gathering herbs and plants at the midnight hour. Near the woodland ride, we discover other signs, particularly in the shapes of the trees that tell of the history of the wood and what it has been used for. The word coppice comes from the French, *couper*, meaning 'to cut' and the most obvious signs of past coppicing is the presence of 'many-trunked' trees growing on the site of old coppice stumps. It was also important in past times to keep livestock out since they would destroy the young shoots and so the area was surrounded by a ditch with a large bank inside, which was often fenced. Old woodland may also have the remains of a stone wall used to protect the coppiced area. In Hunter's Wood, the remnants of the bank and wall can still be seen where the ruins of the charcoal burner's cottage disappears under a tangle of briar and bramble.

A witch should know that the efficiency of the woodland's eco-system depends on how much of the sun's energy can be utilised by the green plants and converted into carbohydrate. The tallest trees of the wood, which form the 'canopy', are the first to receive the sun's rays and what grows beneath this layer depends on how much light can filter through to be tapped by other more lowly plants. In beech woodlands, there is very little, but oak and ash are relatively light shade-casters and a lush growth of plants can exist beneath them. Immediately beneath the canopy will be tall bushes and small trees, which form the second or 'shrub-layer' of the wood.

Growing beneath the shrub layer is a mass of herbaceous plants that form the 'herb layer', so vital to a witch's traditional wort-lore. Many of these plants come into flower early in the year, or have developed large flat leaves to make the most of what light is available. The lowest layer of all is the 'ground layer' of mosses and liverworts, which remain green throughout the year and are actively growing even in winter.

Another clue to woods that were once coppiced is the abundance of spring flowers. The regular tree cutting allowed plenty of light to reach the woodland floor and this encouraged the growth of the plants. Woodland flowers are slow to spread and so their presence in large numbers is an excellent indication that the wood is ancient; bluebells spread very slowly on heavy clay soils, so a carpet of them under trees could also be the clue to old woodland. Primroses, violets and wind-flowers are found here — all part of the medieval witch's medicine chest.

Wild flowers also provide the woods with some of their most attractive features. Because many have adapted naturally to flower before the leaves develop in the shrub and canopy layers, they are regarded as the harbingers of spring. No doubt to our hunter-gatherer ancestors this reawakening of the woodland contributed to the mystical significance of the many rites and rituals associated with the season. A further indication of an old wood is a rich *variety* of flowers, particularly if bluebells, snowdrops, wood anemones, primroses, yellow archangel and early purple orchids are present. Dog's mercury may seem to be a common woodland plant yet it is rarely found in recently planted woods — that is, woodland that has formed in the last 100 years — and so is also a good indicator of old woodland. The presence of such flowers in a hedge also suggests that it originated as part of a wood, since these species do not readily colonise hedgerows.

The deeper we penetrate into the Wood's interior we come to the denser shade of a holly thicket and even on the brightest summer's day, little light filters through the overhead canopy. This part of the Wood is imbued with a strange atmosphere and, as in so many natural places that people have left alone, a witch enjoys the frisson of nervous wonder. The woodland floor is bare except for dried prickly leaves and a scattering of boulders covered entirely in the rich velvet green of a variety of mosses. Here the stems and branches of the holly trees are almost pure silver-white, not the dingy pewter colour of urban trees — and the holly possesses magical protective powers that can be used in amulets and talismans.

Nearby we find an old beech tree that is so hollow it is amazing the blasted trunk can support the massive branches and rich canopy. This once handsome giant of Hunter's Wood is coming to the end of its life but each year it sprouts the delicate veil of green leaves that tells us spring is well and truly here again. In the folds of its hollow trunk, we can shelter from summer showers; eat beechnuts in the autumn and remain safe and dry as the winter snow drifts down through the branches. Whenever we pass this way, we greet the old tree as though it were a friend and hope it survives the next winter's gales.

The Sacred Places

It is said that the forest knows all and is able to teach all; that the forest listens and holds the secret of every mystery.

Since ancient times, woods have been places of sacred groves and nemorous temples, including those of the Druids and Iceni. Sir James Frazer refers widely to sacred groves and tree worship in *The Golden Bough*, while Old Craft teacher, Mériém Clay-Egerton wrote extensively on the subject of trees and produced some highly evocative pieces relating to her experiences:

> *To me this was a place that had obviously been held as a sacred area for so very long now that it had in its turn breathed this very atmosphere itself and so projected this onto a mind which was prepared or conditioned to be both sympathetic and empathetic to various woodlands and their forms of existence … it resembled what I might envisage as a naturally constructed 'cathedral'. Here lived and breathed holiness and beauty …*

The Wild Wood, however, is the dark, untamed part of natural woodland where unearthly and potentially dangerous beings are still to be found. This is not everyone's favourite place and many urban witches never get over an 'atavistic fear of Nature uncontrolled'. Historically, the term 'wildwood' is the name given to the forests as they were some 5,000 years ago, before human interference, and the pollen records for that time confirm that elms made up a substantial component of the wildwood, along with the oak, birch and lime.

On a magical level, the Wild Wood refers to those strange, eerie places that remain the realm of Nature and untamed by man. Ancient gnarled oaks, festooned with ferns and draped with lichen, carry an air of solitude and remoteness that is deeply unnerving — here birdsong and the trickle of running water are the only sounds to break the stillness. It is the Otherworld of the 'unearthly and potentially dangerous'. It is the realm of Pan and the Wild Hunt. In modern psychology, it refers to the dark inner recesses of the mind, the wild and tangled undergrowth of the unconscious.

Here, among the trees, we are never sure that what we see is reality or illusion.

Mériém Clay-Egerton described the strange half-light that anyone who walks in the Wild Wood will immediately recognise. '*I was always glad to go deeper into the apparent gloom because I would be beyond one of the woodland's outer barriers '*

Although it is impossible to describe the sensations of the Wild Wood, no one who has walked there can remain unchanged by the experience.

Nevertheless, even witches are not always welcome in this tree-filled wilderness. Hostile forces can physically bar our entrance into the inner sanctum of the wood, just as Philip Heselton describes in *Secret Places of the Goddess*. The undergrowth is a thick tangle of briar and bramble, giving the aura of a place 'set apart for mysterious concealment'. Entwined with these almost impenetrable barriers, are tufts of tall ferns, the seeds of which can be used to cast a witch's cloak of invisibility. We must learn to heed the signs, however, for Nature does not always allow humans to pass.

Nevertheless, *Traditional Witchcraft for the Woods and Forests* takes us on journeys of discovery through Nature's own woodland 'calendar' and, hopefully will reawaken the dormant senses that coursed through the veins of those witches who lived long ago in these ancient places. In a series of guided meditations and pathworkings, we will learn how to reconnect with the spirit of the landscape and learn to walk softly through the woodlands of both the physical and the astral realms. We will come to understand the gift of Nature's bounty, and make use of the materials that will ultimately lead to an intimacy with wild things that can only come about through close contact and familiarity.

Before embarking on these journeys, however, we need to clarify what we mean by meditation and pathworking. For many witches, the preliminary exercise we refer to as 'visualisation' has become confused with the actual pathworking itself. This often results in those who remain stuck at the 'visualisation level', missing out on the deeper experiences of meditation and pathworking, simply because they do not realise those other levels exist. For the purpose of the exercises in this text, they have been separated as follows:

Visualisation

Controlled thought projection of a magical journey or scenario in which we *consciously* take part. This technique is used by more experienced practitioners as a springboard for pathworking or meditation. In some traditions, this is referred to as actual pathworking, while others use it purely as a relaxation exercise.

As a simple exercise, try to imagine yourself standing in a bluebell wood on a warm, sunny day. The spring canopy casts a dappled shade on the deep blue carpet that stretches deep into the wood like a rippling road we are about to walk along. Start walking amongst the flowers: this is an astral exercise, so you cannot damage the plants. Imagine that you keep walking until you come to a bright forest glade and sit down at the foot of a huge oak tree listening to the hypnotic hum of insects and the whispering of the leaves on the breeze ... enjoy the sensations of the scene you have created for a moment before allowing yourself to come back to the present.

When you have completed the exercise, clap your hands to 'break the spell' and treat yourself to a sweet biscuit and hot drink, since this is the most effective way to disperse psychic energy.

Pathworking

The pathworking is an astral journey for the purpose of gaining magical/mystical instruction whereby the practitioner has *no control* over the outcome or sequence of events. This state is usually reached *via* visualisation where practitioners set the scene on a conscious level, but then allow themselves to be drawn into an involuntary journey of discovery and/or revelation.

... as your mind is lulled into a sense of tranquillity, you concentrate on creating the floating sensation that is required to draw you into onto a different plane. Your physical body remains sitting in the grass at the

foot of the tree but suddenly your astral body begins a journey of its own, and one over which you have no control. You may find that the bluebells have metamorphosed into a swirling vortex of electric blue, or that you have risen up into the leafy canopy high above the ground ... you may even smell the subtle perfume of the flowers ... allow the sensation to run its course but keep alert for any message or sign that is the true purpose of any pathworking ...

When you have completed the pathworking, clap your hands to 'break the spell' and treat yourself to a sweet biscuit and hot drink, since this is the most effective way to disperse psychic energy. Make a note of results in a Magical Journal, although you may have to repeat the exercise on several occasions before the floating sensation kicks in.

Meditation

Achieving a state of mind in which the consciousness is expanded in order to probe the inner depths of the subconscious, to see what emerges from a process of deeper reflection for the purpose of mystical enlightenment. Meditation does not involve a loss of consciousness, simply because there is little purpose in having experiences, which we cannot accurately recall.

... the peace, tranquillity and fragrance of the bluebell wood helps clear your mind of everyday problems and worries. Focus on a single flower, or pattern in the tree bark, and empty your mind of everything else other than this perfect piece of Nature's jigsaw ... see what images or impressions come into your mind, or any solutions to immediate problems.

When you have completed the meditation, clap your hands to 'break the spell' and treat yourself to a sweet biscuit and hot drink, since this is the most effective way to disperse psychic energy.

It should now be obvious why it is important that

pathworking must not be confused with meditation or visualisation. This is an exercise of the Will, whereby the mind focuses its powers on an objective, or idea, until it 'yields its essence'. Pathworking, as a *result* of visualisation, brings mental energy to bear on a certain point in question, so that with its subsequent development, further doors are opened to the mind. Meditation on the other hand does not require any forcible harnessing of the Will because it is something that emerges from the cessation of conscious thought.

But to return to Hunter's Wood ...

Throughout our long history, forests have been places of shelter, providing food for man and fodder for the animals; wood for fuel (i.e. warmth and cooking) and for making weapons and other utensils. Hence, the traditional Craft salutation of *Flag, flax and fodder* .... At the same time they have also been places of fear, where the temperamental Faere Folk, wood sprites and elementals lurk in the dappled shadows — entities with whom the witch must share the beauty of the landscape.

And even today, few places can rival an English oak wood in early summer for peace and beauty with its carpet of primroses or bluebells. Or the cathedral-like majesty of the autumn beech wood with the sun's light filtering through the leaves. Or the brooding quiet of an ancient holly wood. Perhaps it is not surprising that our ancestors performed their acts of homage in forest clearings and woodland glades, for this was where they came face to face with Nature — however they chose to see it.

So ... no matter where you live, there will always be a wide variety of trees in the immediate vicinity, whether open countryside, urban parkland or municipal gardens. Get to know them, learn to recognise the different species, and draw on the magical significance of the Tree of Life. Be humbled in the presence of the trees, by their great size and beauty ... and learn to work with them as a witch.

Practical exercise:

Add several books on native trees to your library, including a 'picture book' of woodland photographs, and a pocket guide that can accompany you on your quest. Familiarise yourself with three trees mentioned in this chapter — the oak, ash and birch. Research the folklore and traditional folk medicine connected with each tree and record for future use.

Magical exercise:

Study the description of Hunter's Wood and as an initial visualisation exercise try visiting different parts of the wood as they have been described. If necessary, use a colour photograph from a book to aid concentration. Make yourself comfortable where you won't be disturbed — either inside the house or outside — and begin to build up a picture of a particular area of the woodland in your mind's eye. Some beginners find the exercise works better if they are holding leaves or twigs from the same type of tree they are attempting to visualise. Imagine yourself walking through the woodland of your choice, following one of the winding paths made by wild animals, taking you deeper into the trees. For maximum effect, try visiting different parts of the Wood at different times. Enjoy the sensation and if you feel that you are being pulled onto a different level of consciousness, don't be alarmed — this is merely the next step of pathworking. If, however, you don't feel comfortable, clap your hands and this will disperse any unexpected psychic or astral links. When you have completed the exercise, enjoy a moment of reflection with a hot drink and a sweet biscuit to 'earth' yourself.

Chapter Two

The Native Trees

Neither the season, nor the flight of time, leaves a mark upon the forest; virgin in the days of which we cannot guess the morn ... virgin it will remain in the days of generations yet unborn.
'The Lore of the Forest', Alexander Porteous

It is perhaps surprising to learn that only 35 species of tree are indigenous to the British Isles. The majority are common native trees that a traditional witch should be able to recognise and utilise for magical purposes. Although strictly speaking the blackthorn and elder are classed as shrubs, their place as sacred or magical trees cannot be ignored, and so their addition brings the number up to 37 that would have been familiar to the native people of these islands.

The following is a general guide to those trees, together with their mythical and folklore associations. Although we won't see them all in the same woodland, we should be able to spot many of them as we walk through different locations during the changing seasons. Some, however, are more common in hedgerows, while others require a more specialised habitat and are much rarer to find. Although these trees have been part of our natural landscape for thousands of years, it is often surprising that some have little related folklore, superstition or Craft use.

KEY

*Included in more detail in the companion volume, *Traditional Witchcraft for Fields and Hedgerows*.

**Trees that have a rare or more specialised habitat.

Alder

In ancient times, the indigenous tribes of Britain regarded the alder (*alnus glutinosa*) as sacred, believing it to possess 'human' qualities when they first witnessed the white wood turning a vivid reddish-orange — the colour of blood — when it was cut. This caused the alder to be revered as a sentinel, guarding the realms of Otherworld. The tree was sacred to the old British god Bran, and incoming deities such as Eostre, while the Norsemen observed *the lengthening month that wakes the alder and blooms the whin* (gorse), calling it *Lenct* — meaning Spring.

The alder was originally one of the seven Celtic Chieftain trees, displaced by the ash following the mythological 'battle of the trees', which suggests that it was sacred long before the Celts came to these islands. It was described as *the very battle-witch of all woods, the tree that is hottest in the fight,* which infers it may have been a military standard or clan totem belonging to the native people in their battles with the invading Celts. The tree also has its associations with the Faere Folk, whom many identify with the native people of the British Isles. The alder was used for its fine dyes: red from its bark, green from its flowers, brown from its twigs — with the green dye long linked in folklore with the green clothes of the Faere Folk.

Left to its own devices, thickets formed by the alder, usually together with a tangle of matted bramble and nettles, quickly become impenetrable to humans, yet provide an ideal habitat for the flora and fauna of the water margin. This demonstration of the alder's continuing battle to reclaim the land that was lost to our native ancestors makes it an obvious candidate for the 'very prince of sacred trees'. Unfortunately, in modern Wicca, and even many areas of traditional Craft, the alder is sadly missing from their tree-lore.

As a good luck charm or amulet, hang a sprig of alder with both male and female catkins near the hearth, together with a small

green pouch containing a silver coin with the image of a head, to bring protection for the family.

Ash

The ash (*fraxinus excelsior*) has long been revered as a sacred and fortunate tree, connected with fire, lightning and clouds. In some pagan mythologies, it appears as an ancestor of mankind, and played an important role in ancient Nordic mythology where it was regarded as *yggdrasil*, the 'Tree of Life' — a huge tree, whose crown reached up to heaven and whose roots penetrated down into Otherworld, and from which the gods ruled the world. In Celtic Ireland, the tree took on a sacred significance and was often the predominant tree 'as the companion of the holy well' — numerous great ash trees or their stumps can still be found at holy well sites. Because of its sacred and magical character, the ash was considered a dangerous tree to cut down without the necessary propitiatory observances. As late as the 18th and early 19th centuries, Derbyshire people still believe that anyone wantonly destroying an ash tree would certainly be deported as a result of misfortune.

Unlike the alder with its Faere Folk associations, the ash is benevolent and friendly to mankind. It cured diseases; it could be used in divination and charms. Its leaves and wood protected all who kept them in the house or wore them, from all sorts of evil — in later times, they were used as a charm against witchcraft! The dividing line between magic and folk medicine can become blurred when referring to old remedies but both would have been the province of the local wise or cunning women, and the leaves of the ash have been used to treat all manner of complaints. Dried they can be taken as a gentle form of laxative, to ease colic, help pass kidney stones and as a treatment for gout, rheumatism, jaundice and flatulence. An infusion of ash leaves in the bath is said to soften the skin.

In Lincolnshire, the berried, female ash was known locally as 'sheder' and used to defeat the spells of male witches; while the berry-less variety, or 'heder' was used against female witches. This belief indicates that the old charm against evil was used long before it was hijacked by the Victorian folklorists. In Devonshire, newborn babies were given their first bath by a fire of ash-wood; and probably the best-known ash-cure is that used in the treatment of ruptures and rickets in children. The rites differ from county to county but there are records of this effecting a cure.

Give a small red pouch of ash-keys to a friend to bring health, wealth and prosperity, particularly if they have children. This should be burned for good luck at the Winter Solstice.

Aspen

One of the most hauntingly beautiful of our native trees, the aspen (*populus tremula*) is also one of our less familiar. Sometimes referred to as the 'quaking aspen' or 'shiver-tree' because its leaves tremble in the slightest breeze, the tree has been the source of adverse folklore, associating this lovely tree with evil and gossip. The aspen is a species of fast-growing poplars that can quickly reach a height of 65ft. It is more common in the northern Britain where it is most often seen on hillsides and valleys, especially where the soil is fairly damp and light. It does, however, grow in hedgerows and copses, and is quite often seen in open oak woods: in Hunter's Wood it can be found growing along the stream flanking the marshy heath.

In Scotland, aspen wood is little used because of the tree's folklore. Geoffrey Grigson, writing in *The Englishman's Flora* comments rather cynically: 'If the timber had been tougher, harder, more durable, and more valuable, perhaps the legends would have been different'. But if the aspen has little commercial worth, it has been much admired by artists and poets. Gerard Manley Hopkins wrote some famous lines in memory of the aspens at Binsey near Oxford after they had been cut down:

> *My aspens dear, whose airy rages quelled,*
> *Quelled or quenched in leaves the leaping sun,*
> *All felled, felled, all are felled.*

To stop gossip and rumour-mongering, wrap three aspen leaves in a small parcel of silver baking foil — reflective side out — and place behind the skirting board in the main entrance of the home to deflect negative energy.

Beech

The beech is one of our most handsome trees; its massive, smooth silver-grey trunk, the delicate spring foliage and vivid autumn colours give it a stature few other trees can match. Despite the magnificence of the beech, however, there is surprisingly little in terms of British folklore associated with the tree, apart from it offering protection from lightning. Although the common beech (*fagus sylvatica*) is classed as one of the native trees of the British Isles, pollen records show that it only arrived some 3,000 years ago compared with other species. There are, for example, many early records of alder wood and catkins dating back 10,500-9,500 years from Yorkshire; while the ash was known to be present in southern and central England between 7,000-6,000 years ago.

Despite their massive trunks, beech trees are shallow rooted, which makes them susceptible to storm damage. If they survive, and beeches will reach 100 feet when fully grown, the beech's normal life span is about 300 years — although some of the ancient pollards at Burnham Beeches are known to be over 400 years old. Other 'hulks' at Windsor Forest and Wyre Forest may be even older. Pollarded beeches eventually become hollow and this enables them to live for centuries, since they are much better equipped to stand up to strong winds.

The beech has always been recognised for a number of medicinal properties, with Culpeper recommending beech leaves as a cooling agent to alleviate swellings by boiling them to make a poultice. In Europe, beechnuts were eaten in times of famine while the nut oil can also be used for cooking.

As an amulet or good luck charm, give a small pouch made from purple fabric and containing three beech nuts to a student, or anyone studying for exams.

Birch

There are two native birches, the downy birch (*betula pubescens*) and the silver birch (*betula pendula*). This was one of the earliest trees to colonise Britain after the last Ice Age with pollen records having been found that date back to 13,500 years, although it is believed to have become very rare or even on the verge of extinction between 11,000 and 10,200 years ago. With its characteristic silvery bark and delicate leaves, it is easy to appreciate why the birch has inspired painters, poets and writers down through the centuries. For example:

> *Beneath you birch with silver bark,*
> *And boughs so pendulous and fair,*
> *The brook falls scattered down the rock;*
> *And all is mossy there.*
> Samuel Taylor Coleridge

Both species produce a bitter, astringent tonic that has diuretic and mild laxative effects; it reduces inflammation, relieves pain and increases perspiration. This can be used internally for rheumatism, arthritis, gout, water retention, cystitis, kidney stones, skin eruptions and fevers. Externally, it is used mainly in the form of birch tar oil, for the treatment of psoriasis and eczema. The sap can also be fermented to make beer, wine, spirits or vinegar and Culpeper recommends it 'to break the stone in the kidneys and bladder', and as a mouthwash.

The folklore associated with the birch is wide and varied since it can be used as a protective charm against evil spirits, bad luck and the evil eye — or for a spell for fertility and love. The birch is one of the Nine Woods of the Beltaine Fire, and makes excellent kindling for campfires as the wood burns well. The tree was also believed to have life-giving properties and in some parts of the country, birch branches were hung over the doors on Midsummer Eve as they were considered to be symbols of return and renewal.

To bring yourself under the protection of 'the lady of the woods', place a few small slivers of the silver bark in a small green pouch, and hang over the door at the Summer Solstice.

Blackthorn*

The blackthorn (*prunus spinosa*) is probably the tree (or more correctly, shrub) most strongly identified with traditional British Old Craft through its long associations with magic and the Faere Folk. Mentioned in Celtic Brehon law, it is even supposed to have its own special tribe of Faere guardians who will take revenge on anyone cutting a branch from the tree at either the old opening or closing of the year.

Archaeological research has established that the fruit from the blackthorn — sloes — which were common in the wild, were consumed in large quantities as far back as Neolithic times. These ancient references probably explain the deep-rooted fear of the blackthorn as something that is best avoided since it represents the displaced, indigenous people of these islands.

The ultimate in protection against enemies on both the inner and outer planes is an amulet made from the sharp spikes from the blackthorn, and placed in a pouch made of black fabric.

Keep this about your person if you feel you are under threat.

Box**

Box (*buxus sempervirens*) is another native tree that doesn't appear in the tree-alphabet despite the fact that it has been around for a very long time. Box grows naturally on limestone and chalk although there are very few places where actual woods of wild box still exist. In 995AD, Aelfric, a Benedictine monk of Cerne Abbas, compiled a list of over 200 herbs and trees in which box was listed. It was used for hedging, topiary work and to shelter young plants.

Although all parts of the tree are poisonous if taken internally (animals have died from eating the leaves) box, taken in small doses, was used as a substitute for quinine in the treatment of recurrent fevers, like malaria. In some parts of Britain sprigs of box were given to mourners at a funeral and then dropped into the grave.

Use box leaves in an amulet for protecting boundaries. Place the leaves in a small brown envelope and reduce to ash that can be scattered around the perimeter of your property.

Cherry*

Surprisingly enough, there are no historical or oral records of the cherry tree (*prunus avium*) being associated with folklore in Britain, although its gum is an old remedy for coughs — hence the traditional cherry flavoured cough medicine that is still available. Although the wild cherry listed by Aelfric is a native of Britain, it is believed that the Romans introduced the cultivated variety. Medieval herbalists grafted the more productive varieties on to the rootstock of the wild cherry and in medieval times, the fruit was picked when it was wine-red, and eaten ultra-ripe.

To create an amulet for a close female friend, place blossom

from a cheery tree in the centre of a small fabric square of cherry red fabric, twist and tie with a green ribbon.

Crab Apple*

The crab apple (*malus sylvestris*) must surely be the real 'goddess' tree of the British Isles. It usually occurs singly, scattered throughout almost all types of woodland and hedgerow in eastern England. According to Oliver Rackham in *Trees and Woodland in the British Landscape*, there were roughly one tree for every ten acres in the 1970s. Crab apples can be found throughout Ireland, England and Wales, although they are less common in Scotland. Although an indigenous tree, the crab apple appears to have been in domestic use since ancient times and crab apples were found in an oaken coffin dating from the early Bronze Age

Place five pips from a crab apple in the centre of a small square of white silk, twist and tie with a silver cord. This will create an amulet or good luck charm utilising female/goddess energy.

Elder*

Although technically classed as a shrub, the elder (*sambucus nigra*) is one of the most useful of our native trees and one of the most widely avoided. For the gardener it is regarded as little more than a weed and both animals and man avoid the ill-smelling leaves; while in folklore it is considered to be a most unlucky tree. For the witch and the countrywoman, however, the elder is known as the 'poor man's medicine chest' having countless uses in folk-medicine.

Elder grows almost anywhere, from heavily polluted roadsides to wind-lashed cliff-tops where it is crusted with salt from the sea spray. It thrives on waste ground, in hedgerows, on heathland, chalk downs, woodland and scrub, and especially where the soil is rich in

nitrogen from the manure of animals such as rabbits and badgers. You often see it near drains and sewers — it can be a sign to archaeologists of the site of former dwellings (The Patchwork Landscape)

Ellen-wood can be used for personal charms to turn aside ill wishing. Place small pieces of the wood in a purple fabric pouch, tied with a white cord and hang around the inside of the house.

Hawthorn*

The common hawthorn (*crataegus monogyna*) thrives on most soils, in open habitats such as hillsides, neglected pasture, on commons, in woodlands and most hedgerows, and has been used for about 2000 years as natural barbed fencing because its tangle of thorny branches makes an ideal barrier for enclosing and protecting livestock. Its name derives from the Anglo-Saxon *haegthorn*, which means hedge-tree and signs of defensive hawthorn hedges have been discovered round the edges of excavated Roman forts.

Hawthorn has perhaps more connections with ancient beliefs, folklore and traditions than almost any other native tree in the British Isles apart from the blackthorn. It is acknowledged as having a powerful supernatural force for good and evil in many cultures. The appearance of the blossom at the beginning of May in the Gregorian calendar (May Day was on what is now 12th May in the old Julian calendar) heralded the end of winter and the beginning of summer. It was said to be unlucky to take May flowers into the house because the Faere Folk are believed to live inside or under the trees — especially those growing on grassy mounds.

To create a charm from hawthorn, collect the buds and leaves from the trees at Beltaine. Using floral fabric, create a pouch that you can keep under your pillow as an aid for meditation and lucid dreaming.

Hazel

The hazel (*corylus avellana*) has always been a major coppice tree and was listed by Aelfric in his *Nominum Herbarum*. It was one of the first trees to grow widely in Britain soon after the last glacial period. In the fossilised pollen records preserved in peat which are our guide to the earliest native plants after the Ice Age, hazel predominates over much of the British Isles — appearing at much the same time as the initial spread of other wind-pollinated trees such as willow, alder and birch. In fact, studies have shown that there was seventeen times the amount of hazel pollen in the air at one point, than the total pollen from all other trees in Britain.

To create a charm for the increase in knowledge place, three hazel nuts in a pouch made from yellow fabric and keep about your person, either in a handbag or a briefcase.

Holly

The holly (*ilex aquifolium*) is probably the most recognisable of all our native trees and is found mostly in parks and gardens and woodland. Holly is also the important evergreen in the traditional pagan Midwinter Festival decorations, symbolising the continuation of life during winter dormancy. The old carol reminds us that:

> *The holly and the ivy, when they are both full grown,*
> *Of all the trees in the Greenwood, the holly wears the crown.*

This is because the holly is sacred to the Horned God in his guise as the Holly King, Lord of the waning year, who takes precedence until the Winter Solstice. It is also sacred to Mother Hel, the Norse goddess of the underworld

Holly is often found in old hedges dating back to before 1700 and across the country, there are relics of medieval holly woods that were widespread in England, Ireland and Scotland. According to Oliver Rackham in *Ancient Woodland*, holly woods appear to have been peculiar to Britain and so for the witch these sites offer an ideal sacred space in which to work. Used as a Midwinter decoration for centuries, it served the same purpose at the Roman Saturnalia and exiled Romans would still have celebrated the festivals of their homeland even if the British climate was a little cold for Roman revels. Because of the tree's pagan associations, the early church attempted to ban its use, but without success.

To create an amulet powered by masculine energy to repel intruders or unwanted guests, place a holly leaf in a leather pouch and hang over the main entrance to the home.

Hornbeam

The hornbeam (*carpinus betulus*) grows as a native tree in the oak woodlands of southern England and is noted for its compact stature and its magnificent yellow and red-gold autumn colours. As the climate became warmer after the last Ice Age, Britain was colonised by trees that spread across from the Continent. The pollen records show that the hornbeam was a relative latecomer, arriving about 5000 years ago, whereas the oak was already widespread 2500 years earlier.

Unfortunately, the hornbeam is not at all well known and may quite easily be passed by as it can be mistaken for a beech tree. In fact, it also goes by the names of horse beech, hurst beech and white beech. The bark of the hornbeam is furrowed, as if with swollen veins, whereas the beech is smooth. The flowers come about the same time as the leaves in April and May and, unless carefully looked for, will not be seen. These are yellowish male catkins, very similar to those of the hazel, while the female catkins are much longer and looser. The fruit grows in bunches and are small, brown nuts enclosed in a leafy, three-lobed 'scale'.

The seeds ripen in October or November and like the beech, the leaves often remain on the tree throughout the winter.

Although there appears to be no references to the hornbeam in folklore, the tree does have a certain rarity value and can probably be credited with the same attributes as the beech as a symbol of strength. Place the fruit with its unmistakable three-lobed wing in a pouch of green fabric and give to someone who needs support.

Juniper

Growing mainly in Scotland and southern England, as a low-growing shrub, except for a few scattered locations in Ireland, north Wales and northern England. In southern England, it grows on the chalk-down grasslands, especially on steeper hillsides where the soil is shallow. In Scotland juniper (*juniperus communis*) is found in native Scots pine forests, birch woods and on heather moorland. On high mountains, it sometimes forms low-growing scrub just above the tree line.

Famed for its medicinal uses, Pliny wrote that the juniper, 'even above all other remedies, is warming and alleviates symptoms'. Roman physicians prescribed it for pains in the stomach, chest and side, flatulence, coughs and colds, tumours and disorders of the uterus. Some even suggested smearing the body with an extract from the seeds as a protection against snakebites. Culpeper recommended the berries for a great variety of ailments. Its country name of 'bastard killer' arose from eating of the berries to procure an abortion

In classical times, the branches were burned as a purifying herb in temples; in Britain, branches were strewn on the floors to sweeten the smell of rooms, and burned to cleanse the air of disease and infection, especially during epidemics. Incense made from juniper leaves and berries would obviously be ideal for cleansing or banishing rituals. (In more recent times, juniper was favoured by those involved in the illicit distilling of spirits because the dry wood burns with very little smoke.) The incense can also be used for divinational purposes for seeing into the future.

Juniper was considered a powerful protection against 'witches, devils and evil spirits' and sprigs should be hung over the doorways at Beltaine and Samhain to keep out any negative energies or troublesome spirits.

Lime

Small-leafed lime (*tilia cordata*) or linden trees are tolerant of most soil conditions and can withstand hard pruning, which is why they are most commonly found in the streets of our towns and inner cities. Although natural lime trees may not be a very familiar sight for most of us, the some ancient limes have a very interesting history and are probably well over 1000 years old. From the pollen records, it is abundantly clear that the lime was the dominant tree species in the forests of England; they reached their maximum extent around 5500 years ago.

Throughout Europe, place names often refer to lime trees with many dating back to the Dark Ages. According to *The Tree Book*, some reflect an earlier reverence for the tree — such as the Roman Tigletus paganorum south of Paris, which suggests it may have been a sacred lime or a grove of pagan worship. In Eastern Europe, votive offerings are still tied to the branches, especially by women 'in search of fertility'.

Today, many ancient limes are found in particularly inaccessible locations, which is probably why they have survived the various forest clearances of the past. Evidence of limes can be traced by place names: for example, Linsty Wood, where the limes were a 'conspicuous feature in the 10th century, as the name contains the Norse elements 'lind' and 'stigr', meaning a path where lime-trees grow (*The Tree Book*). The small-leafed lime trees found in natural woodland also mean that the woods themselves are old.

As the pale timber is prized for use in making musical instruments, it would make a perfect charm for someone with musical interests. Place lime flowers in a square of white fabric, twist and tie with a black cord.

Maple*

Field maple (*acer campestre*) can be found in woodlands and hedgerows throughout England, often growing as an 'understorey tree'. There is very little recorded about it in British folklore and yet again, the tree has been around for a very long time. Pollen records show that around 5000 years ago, the areas of heavy, or calcareous soil, were in all probability, dominated by ash, hazel, maple and elm. Was the maple a sacred tree in England in pre-Celtic times and, like the alder and aspen conveniently over-looked when it came to constructing the Tree Alphabet on which much of today's tree-lore is based? Records trace it back to the Neolithic period and its use as a fodder tree; *mapuldur* was its Old English name. Culpeper recommended decoctions of the leaves or bark for 'strengthening the liver'.

Maple-wood tables were valuable collector's items in the Roman world, one being sold for its weight in gold. To attract wealth, create a good luck charm by placing two gold maple leaves and two coins (one silver, one bronze) in a yellow pouch and hang in the main entrance of the house or business premises.

Oak

From the historical perspective, oak woods covered much of Britain in medieval times and our ancestors quickly discovered that oak (*quercus robur*) made good fuel. From the Middle Ages until the 18th century people drove their pigs into the oak woods on common land to feed on the fallen acorns and such grazing rights still exist in the New Forest. Oak was used extensively for shipbuilding and for supporting beams in country cottages.

The oak has featured in many major folk-beliefs. Sir James Frazer, in *The Golden Bough*, maintained that, 'The worship of the oak tree or of the oak god appears to have been shared by all the branches of the Aryan stock in Europe.' Oaks are part of the sacred triad and it is part of traditional British Old Craft to say that you come from *the Land of the Oak, the Ash and the Thorn*.

From acorns mighty oaks grow: another charm for an increase in wealth (particularly business growth) can be created by placing an acorn in a pouch of green leather, and keeping this close to hand to attract idea and opportunities.

Pear**

The common pear (*pyrus communis*) is now extremely rare in the wild and not universally accepted as being a native species. Oliver Rackham, expert on the British countryside accepts it as such, 'partly because of its widespread occurrence as isolated trees in remote places, which does not suggest planting'. Although the pear appears in Anglo-Saxon charters and was listed by Aelfric, there is very little available by way of folklore. Old single old trees are also found in relics of ancient woodland and pear charcoal has been widely reported from Neolithic sites, as well as being mentioned in medieval documents.

It is said that to dream of a pear tree is a good omen and so place nine pear pips in a small square of white fabric, twist and tie with a silver cord. Place beneath the pillow for dreams and divination.

Poplar*

Modern management of the rivers and riverbanks have eliminated the poplar's natural habitat because this tree is the *last shadow of the vanished flood-plain wildwood*. On the plus side, poplars (*populus nigra*) have been known to regenerate by fallen branches or trunks taking root in the mud to allow suckers to grow from the roots damaged by rivers in flood. Even if it grows where there is no shelter, this tall giant of a tree that reaches a height of 50 to 80 feet, manages to withstand the gales of winter and requires great force to upset it. 'A heavy fall of snow may cover it with a mantle of white and make it seem top-heavy, yet our experience is that it is a warrior and rarely comes to grief except through old age', wrote Percival Westell in *Trees*.

Create an amulet for protection by placing a sliver of poplar wood in a pouch of scarlet fabric and hanging about the door of the main entrance to the home.

Rowan

Traditionally, the rowan (*sorbus aucuparia*) is among the plants offering positive protection against witchcraft and evil. It is reputed to have been one of the sacred trees of the Druids (because it is so often found in and around stone circles). It appears in early Scandinavian myths and its wood was used in the construction of Viking ships, to protect them from harm at sea. While Saxon apothecaries used special spoons made from rowan wood to stir their potions. In Britain there was apparently no situation the rowan couldn't handle:

> *The hags came back, finding their charms*
> *Most powerfully withstood;*
> *For warlocks, witches, cannot work*
> *Where there is rowan-tree wood.*

An old Celtic name for the tree is *fid na ndruad*, or the wizard's tree, as it has a highly significant role in popular magic — hence the Celtic salutation: *Peace be here and rowan tree! The Sacred Trees of Ireland* tells us that sprigs of rowan were 'hung in the house to prevent fire-charming, used to keep the dead from walking and tied to the collar of a [grey] hound to increase his speed'.

Sprigs of rowan hung about the house are considered to bring good luck and to protect the occupants from ill wishing and the evil eye.

Scots pine

Apart from the yew and juniper, the Scots pine is the only native conifer of the British Isles. The true Scots pine, which once formed extensive tracts within the ancient Caledonian Forest in the Scottish Highlands, is considered to be a distinct variety (*pinus sylvestris* var. *scotia*). Pollen records reveal that this pine was the first tree to reappear when the Glacial Period ended. Whole pine trees and pine stumps can still be found preserved under peat bogs all over Britain, mostly dating from the Boreal period, around 9,000 years ago, when climatic changes inundated the land, submerging the trees. In some places, the remains of pine stumps can be found on the foreshore, where the sea level has risen and swamped the coastal forests.

Scots pine leaves, young shoots, buds, oil and tar are utilised in modern herbalism. These properties produce a bitter, aromatic, warming herb that acts as an expectorant and diuretic, improves the blood flow locally and has a tonic effect on the nerves. It is also strongly antiseptic. Pine is used internally for urinary and respiratory tract infections, and gall bladder complaints. Externally it can be used in the treatment of arthritis, rheumatism, sciatica, poor circulation, bronchitis, catarrh, sinusitis, asthma, pneumonia, neuralgia, acne, fatigue and nervous exhaustion. The oil is used in aromatherapy for similar complaints. In addition, the oil and tar are added to disinfectants, bath preparations, detergents and preparations to stimulate hair growth. It should not, however, be given to patients with allergic skin conditions.

As a charm for longevity, place seven small pinecones in a pouch of brown leather and hang outside in the porch to dispel any negative energies and relieve stress within the home.

Strawberry tree**

Of all the native British trees, the strawberry tree (*arbutus unedo*) is one of the rarest in the wild, and can only be found still growing naturally in a few isolated areas in southern Ireland. In its Gaelic form, *caithne*, it appears in several place names. The tree is an evergreen that grows on rocky ledges; it produces fleshly round fruits and bell-shaped flowers that appear in the spring; the Latin name *unedo* means 'I eat one' (and no more!) according to *The Tree Book*. Its bark resembles the matted fur of an animal, and it is one of the few members of the heather family that grows into a tree.

There is little folklore surrounding the strawberry tree, but the leaves and flowers were said to be an antidote to poison and plague!

White Beam**

The whitebeam (*sorbus aria*) gets its name from the white underside of the leaves which comes from their coat of felt-like hairs which help to check water loss — a useful feature on the dry limestone soils on which the tree often grows. In the wild, the whitebeam is found chiefly on the chalk of central, south and south-eastern England. Its main strongholds are the Chilterns, where it can be found in scrub thickets, open woods, clearings and along hedgerows, and the steep slopes of the South Downs.

Despite the fact that it is recognised as one of our native trees, it does not appear to feature in British folklore. According to the entry in *Trees in the Wild*, little is known about its postglacial history because it grows in chalk and, unlike peat, chalk does not preserve pollen records.

The leaves of the white beam shimmer from green to silver as they turn on the breeze; use in an amulet for concealment or disguise by placing seven leaves in a silver foil package (reflective side out) and keeping it hidden about the house.

Wild Service Tree**

The wild service tree (*sorbus torminalis*) is now extremely rare and found only in a few ancient woods, usually on rough slopes along the sides of streams in southern England. The presence of this tree is regarded as an indicator of ancient woodland, although there is little written about it in books on the subject. It is mentioned in the traditional herbals but generally omitted from any texts on folklore, although it was believed to have some medicinal qualities.

The berries were claimed to have health-giving properties, and so a charm for health could be created by placing them in a pouch made from very expensive material, to reflect the rarity of the tree.

Willow*

The earliest record of the willow's (*salix allia*) use by man was in Neolithic times when causeways of willow branches were laid across boggy ground to provide a safe path. By medieval times, in addition to making baskets, fish-traps, fences and coracles, willow was used in tanning, as fodder, to attract bees, to make artists' charcoal, to produce purple dye, and to prevent erosion along the banks of rivers and ditches. The downy covering of the seeds was used as mattress stuffing. In the lowlands all over the British Isles, willows are the most characteristic tree in the landscape, lining the banks of rivers large and small, from the Thames to the Shannon.

To create a charm to attract prophetic dreams, visions and inspiration place a sliver of bark in a pouch of pale green fabric, and place beneath the pillow during sleep.

Wych Elm

The wych elm (*ulmus procera*) is a native tree occurring in woods and beside streams mainly in the west and north of Britain, especially in hilly districts. Historically, elms were coppiced and pollarded and in some counties, enormous old pollards can still be seen. There is, however, considerable disagreement about the classifications and some claim that both the wych and the common elm are native species — but it is the common elm that appears in the medieval herbals.

In modern herbalism, the common elm may be used in lotions for skin complaints but is no longer of major importance since the demise of most English elms from Dutch elm disease. Wych elm, or as it is called in southern England wych-hazel, is also used in a lotion or ointment which is particularly effective against burns. Most modern preparations come from the slippery elm, whose inner bark is stripped from the trunks and larger branches in spring, dried and powdered for use in decoctions, liquid extracts, ointments, poultices, powders and tablets.

Medicinally, it is used internally for gastric and duodenal ulcers, gastritis, colitis and digestive problems in infants. Externally for sore throat, coughs, wounds, burns, boils, abscesses and chilblains. It is often added as a soothing element to cough mixture. Elm was one of the plants chosen by Dr Edward Bach for his flower essence remedies for inspiration. The remedy is made by infusing the flowers of slippery elm in the sunlight for four hours. The dose is four drops, four times a day, under the tongue. Because the bark contains a trace mineral valuable to the brain stem, a tincture of slippery elm has been found useful in treating depression.

Tiny pieces of elm wood placed in a pouch of green leather will give the wearer the gift of eloquence.

Yew

Last, but certainly not least, the common yew (*taxus baccata*) must be the most fascinating and mysterious, if not oldest, of all our native trees. The yew is said to be the longest-lived tree in Britain, some having lived for more than 1000 years. Yew trees are usually solitary but the best place to see them is the famous yew wood at Kingley Vale, near Chichester, which is regarded as the finest in Europe.

Despite being highly poisonous, the yew has always been surrounded by legend and is a symbol of immortality. Many of our ancient yews are to be found in churchyards and if they are well over a thousand years old, then they are more than likely marking sites of pagan worship. With the arrival of Christianity, these were taken over and churches were built to obliterate the sacred pagan sites. Before the advent of Christianity, the yew was looked upon as a sacred tree and a symbol of everlasting life. After that time, the tree was denigrated to mean something sinister or dangerous and to bring cuttings of yew into the home was said to lead to death in the family.

Many ancient yews are found growing on what have been identified as ancient burial sites dating from Neolithic, Celtic and Saxon periods. Studies concerning the alignment of church buildings in relation to ancient yews has also suggested that this indicates the age of the sites and gives a minimum age for the trees. Where the church is west or east of the yew, the site is Celtic; where north or north-east of it, Saxon; and where south of the yew, Neolithic. The yew is one of the Celtic Chieftain Trees, out of which were carved warriors' breastplates, dagger handles, and the sacred brooch worn by the kings of Ireland to be passed on to his successor.

The yew likes limy soil and there is an island on Loch Lomond that was once covered with them, from which bows were supplied, for its hard flexible wood was the best for the purpose. The English longbow was made of yew and some of the oldest weapons that archaeologists have discovered are made from yew and date from the Palaeolithic times — about 250,000 years ago! A yew spear found in Essex was estimated to be some 150,000 years old.

Yew leaves can be placed in pouches of red leather to aid divination.

Guessing the Age of the Woods

Many of the woods that were once pollarded or coppiced are extremely ancient and trackways across the marshy areas of Somerset were built of poles that have been identified as coppiced alder, ash, holly and hazel dating from 2500BC. Trees of many different kinds, with oak dominant, indicates an old woodland; and trees of one kind (such as oak or beech) growing close together with tall trunks and often planted in rows, indicates forest plantation of more than 100 years old. If the woodland is old, it was once either coppiced or grazed.

- If the woods were grazed (i.e. used as wood-pasture) the trees would have been pollarded, so look for old pollards and a lack of variety in ground plants as the clues to old wood-pasture.

- Look to see if there is nothing but grass under the trees. This suggests that grazing continues. Wood-pasture is a dead tradition but some old northern coppice woods are now used for sheltering and grazing sheep.

- Look for signs of previous coppicing: perhaps there are 'many-trunked' trees growing from the site of the old coppice stools. The main point is that a wood that was being coppiced 100 years ago is likely to be an old wood.

- The small-leaved lime is another good indicator, while the Midland hawthorn shows that the old coppiced area has never been anything but woodland.

Britain has more ancient oaks, yews, sycamores and chestnuts (the last two being imported species) than the rest of Europe put together but not all have been recognised as national treasures. The yew is the only British tree to have kept its Celtic name: *Iw*, and the hollowed Llangernnyw Yew is thought to be the oldest tree in Wales. It had survived in total anonymity outside local knowledge for an estimated 4000 years until 1995 when somebody organised a training day for tree wardens, and they came across it by accident! **This tree sprung into life at the time when the megalithic practice of building our ancestral sacred sites (i.e. Stonehenge, Avebury, Carnac), was spreading across Western Europe.**

One of the most curious, is a pair of yews living as one ... the Great Yews of Crom, that stand near the ruins of Crom Castle beside Lough Erne in Northern Ireland. One is female, the other male and by the 19th century they were described as being 'an enormous green mushroom in contour'. Parties of 200 people are said to have dined beneath their branches, which at their peak measured about 23m (75ft) across. Now left to their own devices they spread naturally along the ground. **Believed to have been planted in the 17th century, these trees were alive during the 'Burning Times'.**

Although yews are the longest-lived tree species, others come pretty close. The Westonbirt Lime at Holker Hall in the Lake District is estimated to be 2000 years old, with a girth of 25ft 11in. **A sapling when Cunobelinus (Shakespeare's *Cymbeline*) came to the throne of the Catuvellauni in 1st century BC; he moved his capital to Camulodonum — named 'The Fortress of Camulos', after an ancient British war god (Colchester) — making it the largest and richest centre in ancient Britain.**

In *The Heritage Trees of Britain & Northern Ireland* the authors point out that the ancient oaks are anything but mighty in their old age ... 'being more like wizened old crones'. The most famous trees in British folklore, however, are the 1000-year old Major Oak in Sherwood Forest, said to have links with Robin Hood and standing as a testament to **the times when witchcraft under King Athelstan (935-39 AD) only carried the death penalty if murder had been committed.**

The supposed location of Herne's Oak or Royal Oak in Windsor Great Park was for many years, a matter of local speculation and controversy. It is generally believed that the original tree of Shakespeare's time was felled in 1796 and that Queen Victoria, had a replacement planted on a different site. This new tree fell in a gale in 1863 but the error was corrected by Edward VII, who planted the current Herne's Oak in 1906. **Although modern paganism considers Herne to be derived from Cernunnos, Herne is was a very localised figure not found outside Berkshire and the regions of the surrounding counties into which Windsor Forest once spread.**

The New Forest is the last of the old Royal hunting forests, having gained their status under William the Conqueror. Today, two-thirds of the New Forest are still Crown Land and a sizeable part of this is designated 'Ancient and Ornamental' woodland — almost certainly the remnants of the original forest that covered most of lowland Britain in prehistoric times. Up until the Middle Ages, the forest still dominated the lives of the common people.

It occupied more than one-third of the land and provided them with their livelihood. This ancient woodland — pre-dating 1600 — now makes up less than five per cent of the nation's tree cover but it set the stage for continuing speculation that this was the site of Britain's last sacrificial king. On Lammas 2nd August 1100 King William Rufus set out with a hunting party in the New Forest. Having become separated from the other members of the party, he was found dead having been killed by an arrow. Legend has it that when the king's body was removed to Winchester some 20 miles distant, it left a trail of blood all along the way. **Today, the Rufus Stone marks the site of his mysterious death on this highly significant date**.

What we must realise is that although all trees have an element of mystery about them, not all have *magical* correspondences or associations. Some hints are given in the poem *Trees*, by Walter de la Mare:

Of all the trees in England,
Her sweet three corners in,
Only the Ash, the bonnie Ash
Burns fierce while it is green.

Of all the trees in England,
From sea to sea again,
The Willow loveliest stoops her boughs
Beneath the driving rain.

Of all the trees in England,
Past frankincense and myrrh,
There's none for smell, of bloom and smoke,
Like Lime and Juniper.

Of all the trees in England,
Oak, Elder, Elm and Thorn,

The Yew alone burns lamps of peace
For them that lie forlorn

The witch must learn when to call upon the individual powers of the trees in the Wild Wood and, what is even more important, to recognise the appearance of woodland birds and animals in answer to our magical requests via augury and divination.

Discovering Local Fauna and Totem Animals

Pass further into the wood ... trunks and decaying logs covered in fungi, concealed by brambles, ivy and ferns represent another dead giant, in the process of rebirth. For this 'deadwood' provides essential habitat for birds, small mammals and the insects and beetles they feed on. In old, remote woodland, this process is allowed to continue uninterrupted. Unfortunately, in a large amount of managed woodland and nature-parks, the deadwood is misguidedly cleared away to maintain a clean, safe — but largely uninteresting — landscape. This detritus can be anything from trees reaching the end of their life, those uprooted and windblown branches, to decaying leaves and twigs on the woodland floor.

A covert (pronounced 'cover') is a wood with low under-growth where game birds, deer or foxes can hide; woods named on maps as Fox Covert, for example, will have been the home of foxes for many decades. And a witch's knowledge of this wood-Craft was gained under the tutelage of people who knew how to walk silently in the woods. How to approach a wild creature without disturbing it ... how to recognise where a bird or animal is most likely to have its home ... just how to use the skills with which nature has endowed us in the first place, our eyes, our ears and our limited sense of smell.

Once we learn how to navigate our way in the woodland, we can open our inner eyes and ears, and recognise the creatures that will act as our 'totem' or messengers. A witch builds a sacred bond with what is now commonly referred to as a 'totem' animal and it is important to make this contact as quickly as possible. If we are working within the woodland realm, it is illogical to magically identify with a creature that we cannot expect to encounter in a traditional British forest. After all, we are hardly likely to meet a tiger or dolphin in Epping Forest!

And if we are seeking to empower ourselves for magical work, waiting for the rare sighting of such creatures could cause the moment to be lost! *Carpe diem*! Seize the moment! All animals and birds, and even reptiles and insects, can act as omen bearers and from a traditional witch's point of view, a dog/fox calling, an owl/hawk screeching, or a frog/toad croaking at the end of a ritual, tells the witch that her appeal has been successful, and that the spell has gone home.

So let us return to the woodland and seek out some of the creatures we may need to help us on our path:

- Foxes and badgers prefer to live in woodland, especially where it borders pastureland, and are usually more active at night.

- A particular woodland specialist is the jay, which sports a brilliant flash of white and blue as it flies through the dim light. It is the most handsome and distinctive member of the crow family and you never find them far away from trees.

- The wild deer of Britain were for centuries preserved for hunting in the Royal forests: the two native deer are the red and the roe — the fallow were probably introduced by the Normans. They come out in the open to feed at dawn and dusk; during the day they settle down in a quiet place to regurgitate and digest their food.

- The tawny owl is most in evidence during the hours of darkness, when its exceptional hearing, sensitive vision and noiseless flight make it a particularly effective hunter.

- The two hawks — the goshawk and the sparrowhawk — are the supreme predators of our woodlands. They are swift, silent and deadly in the hunt, specialising in the techniques of close encounter and surprise attack.

- Stoats and weasels are particularly fond of deciduous woodland where there are good supplies of food.

These creatures of the woodland are our guides and messengers and the more we know about them, the easier it will be to interpret their behaviour and learn how to read the essential clues about how they can act as oracles in our daily lives. For example, if you have a burning question or problem that needs resolving, tell yourself that the next 'sign' you see will provide the answer. As with all divinatory methods, to get the answer all we need to do is ask.

Practical exercise:

Invest in a copy of *Fauna Britannica* by Stefan Buczacki. Not only does it contain beautiful illustrations of Britain's fauna, it includes a rare insight into the human relationship with these creatures 'as it has been expressed down the centuries through folklore, custom, tradition, language and literature'. Here is everything you'll need to provide the background information to the creature that you eventually select as your 'totem' animal.

Magical exercise:

Sometimes the totem fauna is recognised when a creature appears to have formed some sort of mystical link with the witch. For example, we might find that if we have a difficult decision to make and, while walking in the countryside, we notice an unexpected daytime appearance of bats, or owls, or foxes — a particular animal behaving out of its normal routine. Alternatively, the image can make itself known by appearing with unusual or distinctive colouring. Often white or albino animals are magical signs and these might appear in meditation, dreams, or even caught for an instant in the glare of the headlights as we drive through the countryside at night. If a creature repeatedly makes itself conspicuous, then we would do well to accept that this may be our link with Otherworld, even if it not something we would normally consider as a personal image. Do not be too hasty to accept or reject such a sign.

Chapter Three

Magical Tree Lore

Even in the city's throng
I feel the freshness of the streams,
That, crossed by shades and sunny gleams,
Water the green land of dreams …
' Prelude', Henry Wordsworth Longfellow

Sacred trees are found in every country and every culture; and even in this 21st century materialistic world, trees have the power to evoke a spiritual response in people, whether or not they are considered to have holy or supernatural connections. According to *The Tree Book*, oak and yew were at the spiritual centre of Celtic, Saxon and other early civilisations in Britain and Ireland, and an important aspect of traditional Craft-lore, both on practical and magical levels, is a sound knowledge of our native trees and an understanding of the natural world that surrounds them. Trees have played an integral part of our cultural and magical heritage, so we also need to familiarise ourselves with the relevant superstitions and lore. Why, for example, do we revere the oak and beech, and fear the elder, alder and blackthorn? Which are the Celtic Chieftain Trees, and which are the Nine Sacred Woods used for the Need-fire?

Much of our native tree-lore has been submerged under a thin veneer of modern fake-lore but for our ancestors, these trees were the focal point of the spiritual nature of the land. In the wilder, remoter places there is still the belief that the 'little' or 'fair people' of the *sidh* (Irish) or *y twlwyth teg* (Welsh) can be contacted via certain trees which must be respected at all costs, otherwise harm will befall those who adopt a cavalier attitude to such sacred places.

Whereas the charms and amulets listed in the previous chapter needed no magical application in their creation — merely a witch's faith in the trees' properties — using the magical energy of individual trees requires a working knowledge of the appropriate correspondences to guarantee success. This is more correctly known in traditional witchcraft as sympathetic magic, a term coined by Sir James Frazer for the principle that *things act on each other at a distance through a secret sympathy* and combining two basic assumptions of magical thinking: mimicry and contact.

Alder

From a magical point of view the alder's habitat of streams and riverbanks, can be viewed as being sacred to **Elemental Water**, although with its various associations, it seems to embrace all four elements. Pipes and whistles were made from alder, making it sacred to Pan and **Elemental Air**; whistles can be used magically to conjure up destructive winds — especially from the North. Associated with the **Elemental Fire** of the smith-gods (because although it burns poorly, it makes one of the best charcoals) it has the powers of both dissolution and regeneration (**Elemental Earth**).

With its pale, flesh coloured timber turning blood-red when cut, the alder can also be seen in symbolic terms of the Sacrificial God and embodying elemental Spirit and, with its Faere Folk associations, the gateway to Otherworld. Primarily, however, the alder is the tree of fire, using the power of fire to free the earth from water and a symbol of resurrection, as its blooms heralds the drying up of the winter floods by the Spring Sun.

Great care needs to be taken when working with alder-power, however, because of the unpredictability surrounding it — as one would expect with anything associated with the Faere Folk. When collecting flowers, cones, leaves or wood it is advisable to leave something in exchange for what you take. Used as incense, alder can be used to disperse other powers and to dissolve malevolent forces. On the other hand, when burnt it can also cause dissention between even the closest of relationships — and the felling of a sacred alder will be revenged by fire in the home. Hang a sprig in your home, however, and alder brings you and yours under the protection of powerful forces, which will both attract good fortune and banish negative powers. Collect this before the Autumnal Equinox when both cones and catkins are fully developed. The dried cones also make suitable decorations to add to Yuletide gifts or as spicy *pot pourri*.

Perhaps it is this unpredictability that makes modern witches shy away from working with alder-power since the tree is neither benign nor benevolent. For serious magical practitioners, however, the uncertainty of working with the alder is part of its irresistible challenge as a 'battle-witch' with all its connotations of ancient ancestral power.

The Power of the Tree
Use the power of the alder in magical workings for protection against enemies, since the wood becomes 'blood-stained' when cut. Blood is one of the most powerful ingredients in magic and the symbolic 'blood' of the alder, and its long ancestral-warrior associations, make it an ideal wood for dealing with serious problems of treachery and violence.

Ash
Magically the leaves can be used in any rites of regeneration — either in incense or as part of a cleansing bath. They are particularly powerful when used in negating magic or charms for protection — either as incense or carried in a charm bag, which works just as well for people, animals or the family car. Ash keys can be taken as a brew to help bridge the void between the worlds; as an aid to divination or scrying; or in a spell for prosperity — particularly if burned at the Winter Solstice. The

wood is used as a charm to protect against vampires (psychic or otherwise) and is known to contain mild treatment against malaria and fever.

Although in modern witchcraft the ash is often referred to as 'the Goddess tree', and associated with the Triple Goddess, this is rather misleading. In classical Norse, Greek and Celtic literature, the ash is seen to have predominantly *masculine* associations. From natural history's point of view, however, the ash can undergo a sex change from year to year; a male tree of last year may be female this year, and perhaps bisexual the next. This means that the tree is the perfect magical androgyny — i.e. its sexual/magical/mystical propensities are interchangeable and that it can be 'both, either or neither'. It is one of the last trees to come into leaf that gives rise to the country rhyme that associates it with **Elemental Water**:

> *Oak before ash, we're in for a splash;*
> *Ash before oak, we're in for a soak!*

The traditional ash-faggot is made up of ash twigs and burned at Yule to ensure good fortune in the coming year. This is another version of the 'Yule log' and a miniature bundle can be kept in the house for good luck.

The Power of the Tree
Use the power of the ash in magical workings for *lesser* protection, harnessing the androgyny of its natural energies, especially when it comes to dealing with an unknown or unidentifiable assailant. Ash keys can be taken as a brew or incense as an aid to divination or scrying to help clarify the situation.

Aspen
The aspen's 'airy rages' have been the source of much local

folklore and legends - although most have a biblical basis. This usually means that a tree or plant originally had 'pagan' associations and so we need to look much deeper behind the latter-day superstitions. For the aspen to receive such 'bad press', it must have figured largely in pre-Christian beliefs, as did the elder (or ellen-tree) which suffered the same fate.

The constant movement and rustling of the leaves has also led to the connections with the sound of gossip and loose tongues. This is recorded in Scotland, where the tree is known as 'old wives' tongues'. In parts of Berkshire it is referred to as 'women's tongue' and the Welsh name for the aspen *coed tafod merched*, also conjures up the same image; as does the Manx name, *chengey ny mraane*.

In witch-lore, *no* tree is looked upon as being 'evil' although each species may have different propensities for averting negative energies. Considering the aspen's name in Anglo-Saxon (*Aespe*) and Old Irish (*Eadha*), and that it is one of our indigenous trees, it would be extremely rare to find little or no mention of it in the old oral traditions, especially as it had some recorded healing powers. On the plus side, the aspen is credited with the power to cure agues and fevers. A very old sympathetic magical charm held that ailments could be treated by something that resembled their effects or symptoms — and since ague causes the patient to shake and tremble, s/he was more likely to be healed by the shaking tree.

In *Folklore of the Northern Counties* (1879), William Henderson records the Lincolnshire belief that to be cured of the ague the sufferer should pin a lock of their hair to the tree and say: 'Aspen-tree, aspen-tree, I prithee to shake and shiver instead of me.' As is usual in many healing charms, the journey home must be made in complete silence; otherwise the magic will be negated. Another method was to bore a small hole in the bark and insert the patient's nail-parings; the hole was then closed up and once the bark has grown over the opening, so the affliction would disappear.

From the magical perspective, the aspen is seen at its best on a moonlit summer night; and when warm breezes stir the leaves, it is possible to believe that this is another tree that might once have been associated with the Faere Folk. The fact that the tree is pollinated by the wind; that its wood was used for arrows, plus the constant movement of the leaves all point to the aspen being associated with **Elemental Air**. Despite its size, it is a short-lived tree and so symbolises the transience of this earthly existence. It this capacity it can be used as part of Otherworld rituals and funerary rites of passage, either included in the incense mix or as a garland.

Since its traditional use was in the production of arrows, it may also be appropriate to fashion the pair that normally decorate the coven stang out of aspen wood. The symbol of the arrow is another connection to the Faere Folk as they were dab hands at archery. Much of what is written here is, of course, pure conjecture, but for those who still possess the spirit of adventure, re-establishing a working relationship with the aspen might just produce some interesting results.

The Power of the Tree
Use the recognised power of the aspen in magical workings for protection against gossiping tongues and slander by creating a miniature arrow from a twig. Obtain a slice of processed tongue from a supermarket and pierce with the mini-arrow — bury both between the aspen tree roots with the command that the gossip should wither on the tongue of your enemy as the meat rots in the ground, or is consumed by wildlife.

Beech
Although there is little in British folklore associated with the beech, the only records of it having a cultural significance are prehistoric — the beech having been of considerable importance

to the various Celtic groups that dominated Central Europe during the Iron Age. It is not represented in the tree alphabet as this pre-dates the time when beech trees became widespread. In *The White Goddess*, Robert Graves' notes suggest that the Franks and the Achaeans originally consulted beech oracles but, finding no beeches on their migrations, transferred their allegiance to the oak, its nearest equivalent, to which they gave the names *phegos* — the same as *fagus*, the Latin for beech.

Beech is also the common synonym for literature, with the English word 'book' being etymologically connected with the word 'beech' from which writing tablets were made. Venantius Fortunatus, the 6th century poet wrote: *Barbara fraxineis pingatur runa tabellis* — 'Let the barbarian rune be marked on beechwood tablets'. Aligned with **Elemental Earth**, magically we can associate the tree with knowledge and learning.

The Power of the Tree
Use the power of the beech in magical workings for the gain and pursuit of knowledge by preparing incense from bark, twigs, leaves and mast. The different stages of growth in the tree represents knowledge at all levels of learning, and the billowing smoke from the incense carries the pursuit of learning to all points of the compass.

Birch
Many different areas have their own version of 'beating the boundaries' which is traditionally carried out to remind a particular community where their territory officially ended. This was a symbolic and magical casting of a protective 'circle' against the dangers from outside and to cast out all negative energies from within the boundaries. Known as 'the Lady of the Woods' the birch is a goddess-tree and therefore associated with **Elemental Water**.

The birch was also associated with corrective powers and in

medieval times, a bundle of birch rods was carried in front of the magistrate on his way to court, both as a symbol of his authority and as a means of correction. Birch rods were used to beat felons (and sometimes the mentally ill) to rid them of the demons causing their affliction, and until recently was still used as a punishment in the Isle of Man.

On a much gentler note, birch is supposed to be feminine and lucky, as the tree of birth and rebirth. Strips of birch bark can be used as a magical writing surface, particular for love spells, while the wood can be used as incense connected with romance. Birch sprigs are also used as garlands to decorate the ritual area, especially at spring and summer celebrations. It is said that birch trees were often used as the May Pole, erected every year at the Beltaine festival and then kept in the stable or farm yard afterwards to protect the household and livestock (especially horses) from being 'hag-ridden', although this is difficult to verify with any degree of certainty. Birch kindling was used to set alight the ritual fire at the rising of the first sun in May to herald the approach of the warmer weather.

The Power of the Tree
Use the power of the birch in magical workings for raising protective energies by collecting a handful of thin birch rods and fashioning them into a long broom-head. Circle the boundary of your home and garden (or land), sweeping all the 'dirt' (and unclean spirits) outwards away from the home, beating the ground and significant boundary markers such as fence posts where it is necessary to change direction, or where there are gateways, etc.

Hazel
Remains of hazel nutshells have been found at the bottom of peat deposits, suggesting that the early Stone Age hunters were probably at least partly dependent on the hazel nuts for food, in

the absence of any sort of cereal. Since prehistoric times the long flexible twigs of 'withies' of the trees have been used to bind bundles, weave baskets, make hurdles and build coracles. In medieval times, the twigs were used for the 'wattle' or panels, in wattle and daub buildings. The brushwood was bundled into faggots that were used for the weekly firing of bread ovens.

The hazel was considered sacred in Celtic mythology as one of the Chieftain Trees, and symbolised fertility and immortality. Since hazel is associated with man's earliest ancestors, it is perhaps not surprising that in Celtic folklore it was also known as the Tree of Knowledge and, as such was supposed to have many magical properties. There are several important Celtic myths surrounding the association of knowledge and wisdom and, like the apple, it was a capital offence to destroy a hazel tree. It was 'the only breathing thing paid for only with breathing things' — meaning that a life would be demanded to recompense for the fallen tree. Irish aches and pains caused by the damp climate — or elfin malevolence — were thought to be warded off by a hazel nut carried in the pocket.

The bark, leaves, and fruit of the hazel had various medicinal uses, including the treatment of varicose veins, circulatory disorders, menstrual problems, rheumatism, haemorrhoids and slow-healing wounds. Culpeper wrote that the nuts, sprinkled with pepper 'draws rheum from the head'. Hazel oil was used for soap and cosmetics, and hazel nuts were a wonderful gift for a new bride — as long as she wanted plenty of children! Incense made from the fruit or twigs can be used for almost all magical purposes, particularly to strengthen mental powers. It is especially effective for aiding magical Will and concentration, also to give the stamina needed to complete long or complicated rituals. Hazel is associated with **Elemental Air** and was one of the nine sacred woods used to kindle the Need-Fire at Beltaine.

Weave a wreath of leaves and twigs to place in your sacred space during magical working to gain your most secret wishes and desires. Most of the spells given in folklore and modern *grimoires* concentrate on love charms but these can be adapted to suit most requests, including banishment. Hazel nuts can be used in love philtres, when they will awaken the recipient to the virtues of the sender. On the other hand, if you want a person out of your life, simply chant repeatedly, *Depart! Depart! Depart!* as you fix their image in your mind's eye and cast hazel leaves into the fire. Hazel nuts can be used to gain the aid of Nature spirits or to make contact with the Faere Folk. Make a necklace of nuts and either wear it when you go into the countryside, or hang it in your home or sacred area to attract the deities of the Greenwood.

The Power of the Tree

Use the power of the hazel in magical workings for divinational purposes especially for asking questions relating to partnerships (business, personal, etc,). Place two hazel nuts side by side on the bars of the fire grate. If they burn together, all is well. If one nut burns, the partnership is one-sided. If they both fail to burn, it could be time for you to be looking to discontinue the partnership. If one or both nuts explode, give it up as a bad job anyway!

Holly

The timber from the tree is white and fine grained, although it is very heavy — even sinking in water. It stains and polishes well, often being used for chessmen, the hammers in harpsichords, the butts for billiard cues and fine engraving. It was apparently used by the Celts to make chariot shafts and, according to Brehon Law, was why the holly was one of the Chieftain Trees. Holly also works well as a protection for domestic animals: fasten some to an animal's collar to keep it safe when away from your protective influences, and be sure to hang a sprig in any barns or stables where animals are kept. This helps them thrive and wards off the attentions of the Faere Folk

When boiled and fermented, the bark makes a sticky substance known as 'birdlime', which was used to trap small birds. This method is often referred to in period novels and history books. The berries of the holly are highly toxic and can cause serious bouts of vomiting and diarrhoea. This can be particularly dangerous for children who may find the bright, shiny berries irresistible. In medical use, the leaves are infused to help to treat colds and coughs, and have diuretic properties that relieve urinary infections. They are also used as a fever remedy and have some therapeutic action in the treatment of jaundice and rheumatism. Despite its many applications, holly should only be used medicinally under strict professional supervision and should never be used as a self-help treatment, or for children. Despite these warnings, many modern herbals encourage the use of holly berries as a purgative. **You have been warned!**

Needless to say, it is unlucky to cut down a holly tree, especially in Ireland where it is also held to be sacred to the Faere Folk. Because of this connection, it is said to be inadvisable to grow holly near the house. In England, however, it used to be planted close to the home to ward off lightning, as well as to repel witches and poison — which according to beliefs of the time, meant the same thing! Aside from good luck that the tree brings when growing near the house, the holly is a weather omen; when the branches are heavily laden with berries, it is a sign of a hard, snowy winter to come.

The wood of the holly gives off a hot fire but burns very quickly. It can, however, be burnt 'green' (i.e. freshly cut), without waiting for it to dry out and is associated with

Elemental Fire.
The kind of holly brought into a couple's home for their first Yule together will dictate who will wear the trousers. He-holly, with the sharp prickles, means the man will be the boss; she-holly

(without prickles or only very soft ones) means that the woman will rule the roost. Some superstitions say this is the way it will be, while others say it only lasts until the next Yule when fresh holly is brought home.

The Power of the Tree

Use the power of the holly in magical workings for keeping intruders at bay, deflecting negative energies and rebounding spells to the sender. On the first count it makes an effective boundary hedge as very few people would be willing to push their way through a holly hedge, so use holly in charm bags and incense for all defensive rituals and, in times of greatest danger, position sprigs of holly around the boundary of your home to keep out negative forces.

Lime

In modern herbalism, the flowers of the lime are used as a sedative, a relaxant, an antispasmodic, a vasodilator (an agent that widens and relaxes blood vessels) and with their mild, pleasant taste, lime flowers are among the most popular herbal relaxants. The flowers produce an aromatic mucilaginous herb that is diuretic and expectorant; it calms the nerves, lowers blood pressure, increases the perspiration rate, relaxes spasms and improves the digestion. Taken as an infusion for hypertension, hardening of the arteries, cardiovascular and digestive complaints associated with anxiety, urinary infections, feverish colds, influenza, respiratory catarrh, migraine and headaches. To harvest lime flowers, pick while they are still young in the summer and dry them for use in infusions, liquid extracts and tinctures. For an infusion: use two teaspoons per cup, infused for no more than five minutes.

Despite the lime's impressive history as an indigenous tree and its multi-layered medicinal uses, it is surprising that the lime does not play any significant part in British folklore apart from the belief that lime flowers cured epilepsy if the sufferer sat under the tree. Perhaps with its associations with healing it should represent **Elemental Air** and also because the Linden Tree was said to be one of the favourite haunts of elves, faere-folk and other beings; it was considered to be unsafe to be near one of these trees after sunset. Perhaps this was because lime flowers develop narcotic properties as they age and should only be collected when first opened. Infusions made from old, stale leaves can sometimes cause sensations of drunkenness.

The Power of the Tree

Use the power of the lime in magical workings for an increase in creativity by making incense from the dried flowers, and burning during a sunset ritual. Have a clear idea of what you require from the ritual as the term 'creativity' can be extremely ambiguous and if not nailed down magically you may get some unexpected (and not always welcome) results. Write your request on a small piece of paper and burn in the incense burner.

Oak

The oak appears to have a great affinity (or attraction) for lightning and is sacred to all storm-gods, such as Jupiter and Thor. The Dagda carried a club made from an oak tree, and the Horned God, especially in his guise as Jack-in-the-Green with his foliate mask (as the god of green and growing things), made up of oak leaves and acorns. In Welsh the tree is called *pren awyr* which means 'celestial tree' or 'tree of heaven'.

Medicinally, a decoction of bark was taken for diarrhoea, varicose veins, haemorrhoids and enteritis, and as a gargle for sore throats. Externally it was used to heal wounds and staunch bleeding. The oak gall (or oak apple) was also prescribed for haemorrhoids, as well as bleeding gums. Culpeper wrote that 'the water that is found in the hollow places in oaks, is very effectual against any foul or spreading scabs'. In modern herbalism the bark is used to produce a bitter antiseptic that reduces inflammation and controls bleeding. It is also taken internally for the same conditions mentioned above, the bark being removed in spring from trees 10–25 years old and dried for use in decoctions and liquid extracts. Acorns were eaten as food in times of famine, and were roasted and ground to make a substitute coffee. The bark and galls are also used in tanning and dyeing.

There is such a wealth of magical lore associated with oak trees that it could take up a book to itself. Both oak wood and the acorns can be carried as amulets of protection — those acorn-shaped pulls on blinds are there to protect the house from evil and lightning strike! Hence the association with **Elemental Fire** When gathering leaves, acorns or bark always leave an offering as the oak is the home of all manner of entities and this will guard against giving offence.

Oak trees have very strong and protective auras that can be used to boost your own physical or mental strength. Approach the tree in an attitude of warmth and openness, tell it what you want and then get as close to the tree as you can. Wrap your arms around the trunk; place the flat of your palms against the bark; or sit down with your back up against the bole. You may be able to feel an exchange of energies, or that you in some way begin to merge with the tree. If the results are positive, keep this as your own special tree — and make some form of payment in return for the energies you've drawn off.

You can also use this special oak as the starting point for outdoor communication with other entities. This special 'relationship' with the tree can open doors to the spiritual and mythical lands of Otherworld. Passing between two oak trees can result in a very profound experience if you are in the right magical frame of mind, as this can take you into another realm of reality. Incense made from oak is reputed to clear the mind and encourage the mental powers. This would be extremely useful for anyone undertaking a period of study or meditation.

The Power of the Tree

Use the power of the oak in magical workings for gathering and developing personal strength: physical, mental or emotional. Since incense made from oak is reputed to clear the mind and encourage the mental powers, use this in a Circle working to draw in the type of strength you need to develop. Repeat the ritual at weekly intervals (i.e. the different phases of the moon) until you feel you have absorbed all the strength you need to deal with your problem.

Rowan

An old Celtic name for rowan is *fid na ndruad*, or the wizard's tree and, according to *The Tree Book*, in Ireland it played a significant role in popular magic. It was hung in the house to prevent 'fire-charming' and in Lincolnshire, rowan twigs were pushed into the thatch and hayricks to stop them catching fire. Both hearths and wells might have rowan placed around them, while it was generally thought that a rowan tree near a house brought both good luck and protection; to cut it down brought misfortune. In England, the tree is either considered to be lucky ... or unlucky. The most often quoted superstition is that rowan crosses were used to ward of the evil intentions of witches, but in witch-lore the little rowan crosses, tied with red thread, were charms to avert negative energies from entering the house.

Rowan trees were also planted near houses to protect them against spirits, especially those of the dead and in Wales, rowan trees are often found planted in churchyards to stop the dead from walking. It is obviously one of those old superstitions that has been 'borrowed' from traditional folklore since those of the Old Ways have no fear of the dead. The belief in the protective powers of the rowan was obviously so strong that the church found it easier to absorb the superstition than suppress it. As a result, most of the folklore handed down through the ages, records the rowan as being anti-witchcraft, when in fact, in representing **Elemental Fire**, the rowan is one of the Nine Woods of the Beltaine Fire.

In Celtic traditions, it was known as the Tree of Lugh, the sun god and was sometimes called *luisiu* which means 'flame', possibly because of its brilliant red berries and orange leaves, which can give the appearance of fire in the autumn woodland. The rowan is also sacred to the goddess Bride, patron of poetry, blacksmiths and healing. Around Imbolc it was looked upon as the wishing tree, when red ribbons should be tied to a berry-bearing branch and the secret wish whispered to the tree. If 'normal' folk used rowan to guard themselves against witches, witch-lore recommends that the same spells be used as protection against other evils. This is where folklore becomes confused because to the church and ordinary people, witch and evil were one and the same. Those rowan crosses used to protect home and livestock, were recommended by witches to protect their goods and chattels from being stolen or damaged by evil intent. Another protective charm for the home is to tie several thin strips of rowan into a hoop that can be hung on an outside wall. This can be made into a decorative wreath to suit your personal taste. Charms bags traditionally contain a miniature stave of rowan wood for protection, together with some of the berries.

The Power of the Tree
Use the power of the rowan in magical workings for dealing with 'unquiet ghosts' by using an infused wash or incense made from the wood and the berries to control disruptive spirits and negative energies in the home. This method can also be used effectively by anyone being troubled with nightmares or disturbed sleep patterns — or hang a sprig of rowan over the bed. This does not apply to vampires, since it was a rowan stake

that was driven through the heart of any undead suspected of nocturnal wanderings!

Scots Pine

The Scots pine has a history of spiritual and inspirational significance that can be traced back to pre-Christian Celtic and Pictish cultures; it is the clan totem of the Grants and the MacGregors. Recent research indicates that Scots pines were planted along the old droveways in the south of England during the 18th century as route-markers during snowy weather. Pine is associated with the Winter Solstice and the rebirth of the sun and associated with the powers of both **Elemental Earth** and **Air**.

The Power of the Tree

Use the power of the Scots pine in magical workings for 'a long life and a happy one' as this is a universal symbol of longevity. The cones, resin, oil and wood can be used in spells and incenses to increase good fortune and fertility/virility but also as a protective element to reverse negative energies. It is also a good addition to any purification ritual.

Wych Elm

Oliver Rackham writing in his *History of the Countryside*, devoted a whole chapter to the tree and observed that elms are: 'the most complex and difficult trees in western Europe, and the most intimately linked to human affairs'. Traces have been found to record that early Neolithic sites showed evidence of elm wood being used for all manner of purposes. Giraldus Cambrensis wrote in the 12th century that the Welsh longbow was made of elm, instead of yew as in England.

In medieval times, the leaves of the elm were used in ointment for burns, wounds and haemorrhoids, and in a decoction for skin inflammations, while sap from the branches was reputed to cure baldness. While Culpeper wrote: 'The leaves

or the bark used with vinegar, cure scurf and leprosy very effectively: the decoction of the leaves, bark and root, being bathed,
heals broken bones'. The inner bark of **slippery elm**, or red elm
(*ulmus rubra*) was used as a laxative and, as a convalescent drink,
to soothe sore throats and intestinal upsets.

The timber had many domestic uses including coffin making.
Elm was one of the timbers used for water pipes, and excavations
have revealed surviving stretches of old mains during modern
building work. Elm piles were laid under bridges and buildings,
including under old Waterloo Bridge and today, when available
is still used in boat building. With all these water association, it
would be logical to assume that the elm represented Elemental
Water but, in fact, it is aligned with **Elemental Earth**.

Considering another name for the tree is *elven*, perhaps it
should not surprise us that the elm is another tree of the Faere
Folk, and that anyone taking the wood should leave offerings of
wine or mead, or small silver coins for them. Because of its associations with elven or Faere Folk, the site of an elm is thought to be
a gateway to Otherworld.

The Power of the Tree
**Use the power of the wych elm in magical workings for incense
that can encourage inspiration and boost confidence. Prepare
your request on a small piece of paper, fold and pass through
the incense smoke; place the folded paper and some small
slivers of wood in a pouch to give the wearer the gift of
eloquence.**

Yew
Pliny wrote that the tree was: 'so toxic that even wine-flasks for
travellers made of its wood in Gaul are known to have caused
death'. While Gerard claimed that the English yew was not
poisonous, he wrote: 'In most countries, it hath such a malign
quality, that it is not safe to sleep, or long to rest under the

shadow thereof'. In medieval medicine, yew was used as a purgative, and to treat heart and liver diseases, gout, rheumatism, arthritis and urinary infections. Culpeper wrote: 'though it is sometimes given usefully in obstructions of the liver and billious complaints, those experiments seem too few to recommend it to be used without the greatest caution'.

Smoke from the burning leaves was supposed to repel gnats and mosquitoes, as well as rats and mice.

Yew is said to be the tree of impending doom, death and, paradoxically, also the tree of immortality. Because yew is representative of **Elemental Earth**, it can aid communicate with earth elementals, particularly those that safeguard treasures — material and magical. It is the tree of Otherworld and one of the holiest in traditional witchcraft.

The Power of the Tree

Use the power of the yew in magical workings for contacting the Mighty Dead since the incense smoke is a perfect aid to divination, or helping to gain answers to questions that can be sought by scrying or the pendulum.

Warning: Incense containing yew should only be used outside or in a well-ventilated room as inhaling too much may be dangerous

The Sacred Trees

In medieval Ireland, under Brehon Law trees were divided into four categories with a scale of fines for their unlawful felling. Many of these references have passed into traditional and contemporary witchcraft via Robert Graves' epic poem, *The White Goddess,* that was originally published in 1948 and became one of the most influential books on emerging paganism during the 1960 and 1970s. For example:

The Seven Irish Chieftain Trees

Oak-*dair*

Hazel-*coll*

Holly-*cuileann*

Yew-*ibur*

Ash-*iundius*

Pine-*ochtach*

Apple-*aball*

As we have seen, not only do the various trees have practical properties, many also have magical associations (or correspondences), and the witch who makes a serious study of wood-Craft will go long way in making that spiritual link with the ancestors and the beings that inhabit the deepest recesses of the Wild Wood. These entities are atavistic in nature, usually appearing in the incarnation of human or animal form of an ancestral being. According to *Man, Myth & Magic*, in a broader sense, the term atavism is used by occultists to mean the reappearance of characteristics which come from so long ago that they 'constitute an embodiment of pre-human consciousness', i.e. things that come from the time of creatures half-human and half-beast.

In Greek mythology, these were more benign beings known as dryads: female nature spirits who inhabited oak trees, although later they were identified with sacred groves and woods in general. The hamadryad was the life-spirit of each individual tree and when the tree died, so did the spirit; they are also found in Celtic folklore and known as *sidhe Draoi*.

The trees that have associations with the dim and distant past are now referred to in traditional witchcraft as the Nine Sacred Woods: apple, ash, birch, hawthorn, hazel, pine, rowan, willow and yew. While the seven traditional Chieftain Trees were apple, ash, hazel, holly, oak, pine and yew, those named in old Irish Law where the unlawful felling was regarded as a serious crime. The trees that should never be burned as part of the bale-fire were alder, beech, blackthorn, elder, lime and oak — but all for different reasons, as we will discover.

Alder Staff or Wand: All Elemental Forces

A witch's staff or wand cut from the alder should be obtained with great care. Since this is a tree under the protection of the Faere Folk, a libation of milk or fruit, and the offering of a small silver coin would be appropriate. Do not underestimate the power of the alder as the combination of all the elemental symbols makes it a formidable wand or staff to wield. Once you have found your tree and agreed a 'price' make sure you take it with a swift, clean cut. Prepare the wood in the normal way but do not allow others to handle it, particularly if used as a staff or stang.

Apple Staff or Wand: Elemental Water

A wand or staff of apple wood would be ideal for a witch who is the leader of a coven because she is symbolically the embodiment of the goddess and also the keeper of hearth and home for the members of her group. Traditionally apple wands were used in all forms of love magic and when selecting a branch to cut, make sure that you leave a libation of apple juice or cider by way of thanks.

Ash Staff or Wand: Elemental Water

According to country-lore, snakes cannot stand ash and will keep well away from anyone carrying a staff made from it despite the fact that it is the tree of Mercury, whose symbol is the caduceus! All deities associated with the ash appear to have a penchant for magical illusion and so an ash wand would be useful when used by a witch for glamouring or enchantment. In traditional Craft, both the coven and personal stang (or staff) was cut from an ash tree as this represents the Horned God. Dressed with garlands and with crossed arrows, the staff was used as an altar, although a personal staff should be left plain. According to Evan John Jones in *Witchcraft — A Tradition Renewed*, 'When an ash staff is found, you will know it is the one for you. It will feel right to the hand. A slight tingling in the fingers will tell you that it is yours and yours alone ... When taking the staff, a small coin is left behind as payment.'

Beech Wand or Staff: Elemental Earth

It is rare for beechwood to be used as a witch's staff or wand but it is by no means taboo simply because the tree was omitted from the tree-alphabets. As the tree has connections with knowledge and learning, it makes it an obvious choice for those witches who pursue their magical quest on a more intellectual level. To obtain a staff of a suitable thickness may prove to be difficult, however, since the branches if the required thickness may well be out of reach. The offering or libation would also need to be something decidedly elevated — such as vintage port or matured malt whisky!

Birch Staff or Wand: Elemental Water

This is a sacred shamanic tree and so witches should carry a birch wand or staff to aid their journeys in this world and through the astral planes: the place of the birch staff within magical rites is that of the bridge between the worlds. The handle of the witches' broom is, of course, a form of staff, cunningly concealed as a simple domestic implement, although this is the *male* component of the besom, often with a phallic shaping to the handle at one end, it is fashioned from alder, ash or birch. The actual brush part of the besom is symbolic of the female component that is made up of certain twigs, including the birch, hazel and broom.

As can be seen, there are so many different facets to the birch tree that it would be a mistake to attempt to pigeonhole its energies merely for convenience sake, or to fit in with any preconceived ideas about tree magic. A light wine would make an ideal offering in payment for your wand or staff, especially if the wine had been made from birch sap.

Blackthorn: Staff or Wand: Elemental Earth

The blackthorn used as a magical tool has long been associated with cursing. According to Evan John Jones:

> As it is a wood of ill omen, the only use of the blackthorn stang is in the solemn rite of a formal cursing when the coven has to defend itself, or one of its members against an attack from the outside. In this guise, it is the representative of the Two-Faced God. From the same stem comes the power that can be used for both good and evil; a face that should be rarely invoked or worked.

Mention of a blackthorn rod has featured in several witch trials that when the body of the witch was burned, their blackthorn staff was thrown into the pyre.

Having said that, there are a number of Old Craft witches whose personal wand is made of blackthorn because this also represents the energies of the god in his dark aspect — in other words the deep, primordial powers of the Wildwood. As with all magic, the power is neutral and the responsibility must therefore rest with the individual and the end for which it is being used. Blackthorn *is* notoriously difficult to control but it should not be viewed as having a sinister or evil reputation. An ideal offering in payment for a piece of its branch would be a handful of dried fruit, or a libation of sloe gin.

Elder Staff or Wand: Elemental Water

Because of the nature of the tree, it is unwise to use the wood for any purpose other than medicinal. Also, on a practical level, the wood in not very strong when dried.

Hawthorn: Staff or Wand: Elemental Fire

Hawthorn is said to be sacred to the powers of Elemental Fire and any demon or malevolent spirits can be controlled with a wand of hawthorn. This is one of the trees of the *White Goddess*, Cardia who casts her enchantments with a hawthorn wand. A witch using hawthorn for a wand or staff must be prepared for plenty of magical surprises because of the tree's associations with the Faere Folk. Make sure to leave a suitable offering if you take any wood from the tree — perhaps bread or cheese.

Hazel Staff or Wand: Elemental Air

Although we think of the forked hazel twig as the diviner's rod, these days a straight hazel wand can also be used for water divining and to attract rain, despite the fact that it represents Elemental Air. A witch can protect a seedbed from the birds, insects and the Faere Folk, by drawing an equal-armed cross, followed by a heart and another cross, with a hazel wand.

Because of its magical powers associated with wisdom and divination, the wood was also used to make a sorcerer's wands and is 'the proper wood for a rod of power'. The most potent hazel wand should be cut on a Midsummer's morning and the carrying of a hazel wand conferred not only wisdom, but the power of eloquence on the bearer. Leave an offering of sweet bread flavoured with nuts.

Holly Staff or Wand: Elemental Fire

Holly wood makes an excellent staff or wand because it is an undiluted symbol of male energies. When out walking at night, a holly staff will keep a witch safe from all mischievous entities, and at one time, no coachman would drive after sunset unless the handle of their whip was fashioned from holly wood. A wand made out of holly is also helpful in keeping unruly spirits under control. An offering of spiced wine might be appropriate if the staff or wand is cut at Winter Solstice.

Lime Staff or Wand: Elemental Air

One of the oldest indigenous trees of Britain, the timber is prized for its pale colour and suitable for carving, turning and musical instruments. Cut the staff or wand as a gift for a witch who is a healer as the tree's beneficial properties are of paramount importance. Pour a libation of a linden flower infusion sweetened with honey.

Oak Staff or Wand: Elemental Fire

A witch's wand or staff of oak is ideally used for personal protection — especially if you are suffering the attentions of unwanted entities. Charged regularly with Circle energy, use the wand to draw a protective circle around yourself, and you will be perfectly safe. A libation of mead would be appropriate.

Rowan Staff or Wand: Elemental Fire

Rowan always works best in a personal way because it responds best if frequently handled. It is therefore the ideal wood to choose as the handle of a witch's magical knife, or to cut for a staff or wand. It is also used instead of hazel for dowsing, while cattle herders cut their droving stick from rowan wood in the belief that it would fatten their animals. Leave some rowan jelly in thanks for your gift.

Scots Pine Staff or Wand: Elemental Earth and Air

Strongly associated with the powers of both Elemental Earth and Air, a witch's wand or staff made from its wood can be a powerful aid when pathworking in the spiritual winter forests and with the Wild Hunt. The wood makes a sturdy protective staff to ward off all negative entities and vibrations. A resinous wine would make an ideal libation.

Willow Staff or Wand: Elemental Water and Fire

Known as the 'Tree of the Ancestors' because it has always been associated with sorrow and lost love, while those who wished to learn eloquence or be granted prophetic visions frequented groves of willow. Willow is one of the woods from which to make the traditional witch's magic wand or staff. This should be cut from the tree with a single blow, having first asked the tree for permission and made a suitable offering. Shaman, sorcerers and enchanters were all said to favour willow wands because it can command the spirits of the dead and its use is a thrown-back to pre-Christian times when willow was acknowledged as being the 'badge' of the cunning man or woman. In Ireland the 'sally' or goat willow has the power of enchantment, and it was lucky to take a sally rod (staff) on a journey.

Yew Staff or Wand: Elemental Earth

A staff or wand of yew should be treated with great care as it acts as a bridge between the worlds. Because it is the tree of weaponry, it has a martial aura to it and very often the only payment for taking yew wood is blood. A pinprick will be sufficient and it is a price worth paying. Rods or staffs of yew are associated in legend with many magical powers and used as a dowsing rod; the yew can lead the bearer to recover missing treasure or property. A witch working with a yew staff or wand must be prepared to constantly encounter Otherworld influences.

In Gaelic legend, the 'white wand' was a special tool cut from yew which gave the bearer incredible magic powers, being associated with the 'spell of knowledge' — a magical working to give the enquirer access to Otherworld and the realms of Faere. Unfortunately, this could also lead to the death of the enquirer. The Scots believed that a man could denounce an enemy while holding a yew wand and prove his case because those hearing his complaint would be able to see he was telling the truth.

With its Otherworld connections, yew was also a protector of the spirits of the dead and carved yew wands were often placed in the coffins of country burials — this later became a belief that it would prevent the dead from walking.

The Sacred Flame

Wood, fire and magic are almost synonymous with each other in traditional witchcraft and twigs from many of these sacred trees should be collected, made into small faggots (bundles) to be burned to ensure good fortune. Depending on the type of magical working undertaken, one should stand in the hearth for a year, and then be burned when we bring in the next year's faggot, to ensure that our good fortune continues. On a practical level, our ancestors would also have known which of the trees could be relied upon to produce a good fire as reflected in this old country rhyme:

Beechwood fires are bright and clear.
If logs are kept a year;
Chestnut only good they say,
If for long it's laid away;
Make a fire of elder tree,
Death within your house shall be;
But ash new or ash old
Is fit for Queen with crown of gold.

Birch and fir logs burn too fast,
Blaze up bright and do not last;
It is by the Irish said
'Hawthorn bakes the sweetest bread'
Elmwood burns like churchyard mould -
E'en the very flames are cold;
But ash green or ash brown
Is fit for Queen with golden crown.

Poplar gives a bitter smoke,
Fills your eyes and makes you choke;

Apple wood will scent your room
With an incense-like perfume;
Oaken logs, if dry and old,
Keep away the winter's cold;
But ash wet or ash dry
A King shall warm his slippers by.

Many traditional witchcraft customs survive from the old pagan fire festivals held in honour of the Sun. These include the bonfires that still burn all over England every Guy Fawkes' Day, which hold memories of the rites associated with the Midwinter Festival and Celtic *Samhain* when fires were lit to strengthen the winter sun. Not to forget the fire ceremony of *Up-Helly-Aa* held in Shetland on the last Tuesday in January, and the chain of bonfires which blaze every Midsummer across Cornwall. . The old saying of *being caught between the bel-fires* (i.e. a dilemma), refers to the two Beltaine fires that were kindled in every village, between which all men and livestock were compelled to pass.

Bonfires were traditionally lit on annual occasions in Wales, right up until the 1900s and Marie Treveloyan in *Folklore and Folk Stories of Wales* writes that Beltaine fires (lit on May Day Eve) were remembered in the Vale of Glamorgan until the turn of the 20th century, when oatcakes were eaten around the bonfire. St John's Eve (the old Midsummer Festival) was also marked by a bonfire; as was All Hallows Eve (Samhain — 31st October). On all occasions, malevolent spirits were thought to be abroad and various plants such as St John's Wort, or woods such as birch, were picked and burned to drive away evil forces. A photograph dating from 1841 suggests that the Samhain fire may have been burned to consume an elaborately dressed 'corn maiden' or *caseg-fedi* (harvest mare) made from the last stook of corn to be harvested. After the bonfire, a harvest supper was served before the dancing and beer drinking for the harvest workers.

Apart from these community fire festivals, traditional witchcraft also uses fire to enhance and empower more private magical workings. The balefire for example, is a ritual coven fire, where rowan is used as an ingredient to attract helpful spirits and other entities, and for shamanic working. While need-fire or elf-fire is a ritualised form of fire lighting that was used during times of distress or poor harvest. The need-fire, or 'living- fire' cannot be taken from an existing flame but must be re-kindled anew without the use of metals. The nine sacred woods of the balefire were ash, birch, yew, hazel, rowan, willow, pine and thorn and any other indigenous trees recognised as being traditionally sacred may be used, **with the exception of the alder, beech, blackthorn, elder, lime and oak.**

Alder, beech and oak were used under special circumstances for a need-fire. For example, oak was the sacred wood burnt by the Druids for the midsummer sacrifice, kindled by rubbing together two oak sticks. Birch kindling was used in Scotland to set alight the ritual fire at the rising of May's first sun, the traditional start to the warmer half of the year. The fires of Vesta, Roman goddess of hearth and home, were kept eternally burning, fed by oak. Magical need-fires are also started with a brand of burning oak; while the Norse Yule log lit at the Winter Solstice (a piece of which should be kept to light the next year's fire) was oak.

On the 30th of April is the time to collect the nine traditional woods for the Beltaine fire, these again being ash, birch, yew, hazel, rowan, willow, pine and thorn or any other indigenous tree **with the exception of oak and elder**. Known as the 'poor man's medicine chest', the elder has a great many positive qualities, but it will bring bad luck to those who cut the wood and take it into the house, or attempt to burn it.

The availability of different trees will of course vary from area to area. If a bonfire isn't a feasibility, collect a selection of appropriate twigs and make them into a faggot (bundle) for burning in the hearth, or in a patio fire. Traditionally, however, this festival would not take place until the May (or hawthorn) blossom was out and during a cold spring, the flowers may not appear until well into May, so much depends upon whether the seasons are early or late rather than any set civil calendar.

Just as fire is regarded magically as something that 'fixes' a spell, or has the power to regenerate and bring new life, so the same properties are associated with the residue of fire — the ashes. Ashes from a magical working should *never* be discarded willy-nilly, but should be retained in order to re-affirm the magical working at a later date. The only truly safe means of disposal is to tip them into running water, unless it is appropriate to sprinkle them around the boundary of your property.

Practical exercise:
Find and prepare your own magical staff or wand from one of the sacred woods that has an affinity with your own magical persona. Ask permission from the tree and cut the branch as quickly as possible, using secateurs or a small saw ... do not rip a branch from the tree and remember to leave a suitable offering in its place. Take the branch home and trim off any twigs before putting it away somewhere safe to dry. Once the wood is dry, you can decide whether to strip the bark and decorate to your own design, or leave it natural. Providing no one else has handled the staff (or wand) magical cleansing will not be necessary, as it will still carry the essence of the parent tree.

> **Magical exercise:**
> Magical practitioners have always made use of secret alphabets and this one can be used for private notes and messages or, if burned or painted onto roundels of birchwood, can be used for divination. The roundels can be produced from branches of birch about two inches in diameter and carefully cut into pieces half an inch thick. Once dried, each piece should bear either the individual letter, name, or both of the tree it represents, i.e. *B* or *Beth* for Birch. If you are unable to make the roundels from wood, stiff cardboard would be a suitable substitute.

The Tree Alphabet

Beth	**B**	Birch
Luis	**L**	Rowan
Nion	**N**	Ash
Fearn	**F**	Alder
Saille	**S**	Willow
Uath	**H**	Hawthorne
Duir	**D**	Oak
Tinne	**T**	Holly
Coll	**C**	Hazel
Muin	**M**	Vine
Gort	**G**	Ivy
Pethboc	**P**	Dwarf Elder
Ruis	**R**	Elder
Ngetal	**N G**	Reed
Ailm	**A**	Scots Pine or Elm
Onn	**O**	Furze/Gorse (or Broom)
Ur	**U**	Heather
Eadha	**E**	Aspen
Idho	**I**	Yew

This version appears in *The White Goddess* to which Robert Graves also added:

Quert **Q/CW** Apple/Quince
Straif **SS/Z** Blackthorne
 Y Mistletoe

The last being magical to the Celts. The Apple is the Silver Bough; the Mistletoe (too holy to have a written letter or name) is the Golden Bough; and the Blackthorn is the tree of Magic and the Faere Folk.

For divination draw three roundels and place in a row. The first drawn is placed in the centre, the second to the left and the third to the right. Each roundel will have its own spiritual and temporal associations with that particular tree, as well as magical correspondences. The central roundel represents the basic response to the question; the roundel on the left represents the spiritual/intellectual influences; while the roundel on the right refers to the earthly/practical side of things.

Chapter Four

The Changing Seasons

Into the blithe and breathing air,
Into the solemn wood,
Solemn and silent everywhere!
Nature with folded hands seemed there,
Kneeling at her evening prayer!
Like one in prayer I stood.
'Prelude', Henry Wordsworth Longfellow

The burning of different woods has been part of magical and religious practice for thousands of years, and within traditional witchcraft this is no exception. All our native trees have differing magical correspondences and learning to identify these within Hunter's Wood, will provide us with a valuable aid to our magical working — i.e. oak for strength, pine for longevity, yew for Otherworld experiences and so forth.

The smell of burning wood is extremely evocative: the fragrance of wood smoke drifting between the trees on a summer's evening ... burning leaves on a crisp autumn day ... so no wonder that a witch uses these *natural* materials for incense. Begin by preparing a series of large coffee jars: one for each of the mature native trees in the vicinity. The jars should be washed, dried, labelled and a fold of kitchen towel placed in the bottom to extract any excess moisture from the wood.

Collect the ingredients from each tree or shrub separately so that the natural energies don't corrupt each other. Pick up small twigs and leaves at any time of the year; the fruit when in season. Place in a cool, dry place until the ingredients are completely dry and then store in the appropriate jar, although the type of fire at our disposal, will influence the method of preparation. If we have an open hearth or outside patio burner then we can use short twigs of between four to six inches in length made into small 'faggots' or bundles in accordance with the type of ritual we wish to perform. For example:

- **Nine sacred woods:** ash, birch, yew, hazel, rowan, willow, pine and thorn.
- **Need-fire:** a single or blend of woods appropriate for your personal 'need' or totem tree.
- **Spell-casting:** a single or selection of woods with the appropriate magical correspondences to influence the outcome of the spell or charm.

To prepare incense for burning, cut the material into tiny pieces that will ignite immediately. The safest way of burning is using charcoal discs containing saltpetre, which lights easily, although we can still burn incense in the flames of any fire, for example, a ritual bonfire, hearth or patio fire. Charcoal discs must be used on a heat resistant surface or proper thurible as they generate a lot of heat. In order to light the disc it should be held over a naked flame such as a match or a candle — using tongs to do this as the disc becomes *very hot very quickly*! The disc will spark and smoke and we can see the ignition taking place as a band of sparks rush across the surface of the disc. When an area is glowing red, the disc is ready to be primed with appropriate incense.

So … let us return again to Hunter's Wood and begin to identify the trees and plants that we can use for magical purposes:

Winter Solstice
Rooky Wood: Not a wood where rooks congregate, but a misty or dark wood. 'Light thickens, and the crow/Makes wing to the rooky wood.' Shakespeare, *Macbeth*, iii, 2.

Astronomically taken to be the period from the Winter

Solstice to the Vernal Equinox (occurring around 22nd December and 21st March respectively in the northern hemisphere) and the coldest, darkest time of the year, when nature sleeps. Hibernation is the only means of survival for some animals during the winter months, when food is scarce and temperatures fall, **but for the traditional witch, winter is still a time for wonder and magic ...**

As John Audley wrote in *Country Illustrated* magazine: 'Nature does not lose her good looks [in winter] ... they merely change.' He was referring to the fact that here in the chill, monochrome British woodland, we have the opportunity to experience and enjoy a different kind of light, coming through the trees at odd angles, enabling us to see the world differently. Winter light has more variety than in summer, with its subtle shades of grey and green and brown. We are privy to pale, liquid dawns and fiery sunsets; low, rain-filled clouds in all shades of grey; gossamer-fine mists; glittering white hoare-frosts; sunshine that is pale yellow and luminous, or brilliant in a deep blue sky, **but for the traditional witch, winter is still a time for wonder and magic ...**

In 2010, for example, the Winter Solstice coincided with a full moon *and* a lunar eclipse, making it a very magical time that will not occur again for another 400 years! Everywhere was a winter wonderland of fire and ice as the morning sun appeared over the brow of a distant hill; sloping orange rays, like tongues of flame spreading between the trees, setting the whole wood aglow. A solitary goldfinch gave out a high, 'tinkling twitter, reminiscent of Japanese windbells'. Traditional witches would have been conscious of this natural phenomena and made use of the highly charged tides that influence that holy time of the year: **a time for wonder and magic ... a physical manifestation of the power of the unconquered Sun.**

There are few witches who do not feel a great affection, almost a reverence for old trees — some being mere saplings when wolves and wild boar still roamed the woodland. And the woods in winter also remind us that we should not confuse the natural with the wild. Our island has not been 'wild' since long before the Romans arrived, and although we may not always do what is right by Nature, the traditional witch is part of it, not set apart from it. Down through the centuries witches have learned to live in harmony with our landscape, for better or worse, in each and every season.

Snow

No breath of wind,
No gleam of sun —
Still the white snow
Whirls softly down —
Twig and bough
And blade and thorn
All in an icy
Quiet, forlorn.
Whispering, rustling,
Through the air,
On sill and stone,
Roof — everywhere,
It heaps its powdery
Crystal flakes
Of every tree
A mountain makes;
Till pale and faint
At shut of day,
Stoops from the West
One wintry ray.
And, feathered in fire,
Where ghosts the moon,
A robin shrills
His lonely tune.
WALTER DE LA MARE

When the snows do come and the slate-grey skies herald further squalls of sleet and snow, the witch will still be out in Hunter's Wood. Here is a glimpse of 'Otherworld' where only the piping song of the robin or the sound of a woodpecker rapping in the depths of the wood breaks the silence. Deeper into the holly wood, the Otherworld sensation is magnified as the thick branches of the holly filter the snowfall and silence prevails. Here the leaves murmur in the cold breeze to tell us that under the blanket of snow, the heart of Nature is beating as strong as ever.

Take this opportunity to step over into Otherworld and use the natural psychodrama of the eerie silence to carry you through. Find a sheltered spot and make yourself comfortable. If possible, sit with your back to the bowl of an old tree so that you can begin to feel the pulse beat that reaches down into the earth. After a time the pulse of the tree and your own will synchronise. This is the gateway where physical and mystical Nature becomes inseparable; it is what we mean when we refer to the 'Wildwood experience'. When the time comes to return home, leave some small token of thanks behind in the form of food for the woodland creatures.

But first, to begin to find our way about the woods, we need to be able to identify the different trees that grow in our vicinity. On young trees the bark is smooth and thin but as the tree grows and fresh layers of bark are formed; a pattern of ribs of fissures develop which varies from tree to tree and, with the colour differences, helps us with identification. The best time to begin is during the winter with Nature offering us a blank canvass — when deciduous trees, stripped of their summer greens and autumnal tints, stand bare and exposed. Wintertime is the season in which we can see the true structural beauty of the trees — a sight that is concealed by foliage during the greater part of the year. For those who wish to know more about trees, their season does not begin in the spring but now, while bole and branch are clearly defined. We need to seek out the 'Old Ones' of the forest and leave the younger trees to the next generations of witches.

Here are three of the most easily identifiable to begin:

The **common ash** (*fraxinus excelsoir*), native to Britain and most of Europe, is widespread throughout the country in oak woods, copses, in hedgerows and along riverbanks. Recognising the ash is easy because in winter the sturdy grey twigs are covered with jet-black, velvet buds; the bark of the mature ash is deeply furrowed with age. The ash is one of the latest trees to burst into leaf and is not usually fully covered until May. The ash loses its leaves quite early in autumn and are frequently shed at the first hint of frost, although bunches of ash keys last well into the winter to provide food for the birds. The name of ash 'keys' dates from medieval times when door keys were fashioned in the shape of the seedpods of the ash tree.

Ash has always been highly prized for firewood because it burns 'green', that is unlike many other woods, it is suitable for hearth fires when it has been freshly cut. Another advantage of ash timber is that it is so tough and elastic that it can withstand stress, strain and sharp knocks and so throughout history it has been used for tools and weaponry, especially for the shafts of spears and lances. The Anglo-Saxon word for ash is *aesc*, which was also used to mean 'spear'.

If you have an affinity with the ash (which Nordic mythology regards as the 'Tree of Life') then find what appears to be the oldest ash tree in the green wood and spend time familiarising yourself with its cycle throughout the seasons. Use the twigs, leaves, bark and keys in your magical and path-workings, and its correspondences for spell casting and divination.

Everyone recognises the **silver birch** (*betula pendula*) with its narrow trunk, silvery bark and slender branches, ending in a mass of drooping twigs that have the outline of a cascading fountain. In winter the ends of the twigs are thickened by stiff catkins, with the bark gleaming ghostly in the half-light of the mid-winter woods. The common bunching of small twigs is a growth deformity called 'witches' brooms' — since the traditional besom is often made from bundles of birch twigs and is similar in appearance.

Not only is the birch a native to Britain, it was the first tree to follow the melting Ice Age and the name birch comes straight from Old English — place names containing 'birk' are scattered everywhere. The thin paper-like strips automatically shed by the tree can be used in spell casting and divination.

If you have an affinity with the birch (described by Coleridge as the 'Lady of the Woods') then find what appears to be the oldest tree in the green wood and spend time familiarising yourself with its cycle throughout the seasons. Use the leaves, bark and twigs in your magical and pathworkings, and its correspondences for spell casting and divination.

The only real colour in the winter wood comes from the **holly** and the ivy, which need no introduction. The holly is one of Britain's few native evergreen trees, and has adapted in curious ways as an undershrub in woods throughout the land. The trees are either male or female: both have the pretty white, waxy flowers in May but only the female develops the bright red berries that ripen by October. These flowers first appear when the tree is around 20 years old but the splendid display of scarlet berries on female trees do not occur until the tree has reached 40 years. Despite being poisonous to humans, the berries sustain the local bird population through the winter when other food is hard to come by. For a variety of reasons, the berries stay on the tree longer than on others and do not spoil or fall off, even after a severe frost. Very often, we will find individual holly trees being vigorously defended by a pair of thrushes who seem to treat the tree as their own private larder.

If you have an affinity with the holly (described as the 'Tree of the Holly King') then find what appears to be the oldest tree in the green wood and spend time familiarising yourself with its cycle throughout the seasons. Use the leaves, bark and berries in your magical and path-workings, and its correspondences for spell casting and divination.

The traditional witch also gives respect to the ivy, which bears greenish-yellow flowers in October, developing into purplish-black berries in the spring. Ivy, like the holly was believed to have magical powers, and during the winter, it benefits from sunlight filtering through the leafless boughs overhead. It also adds a splash of colour to otherwise leafless woods and while various plants may compete for the title of first flowering of the year, the flowers of the ivy are the last to appear, reversing the order of normal seasonal growth.

The custom of 'wrenning' or 'hunting the wren' is one of those old New Year rituals that survived from ancient times right up until the 20th century. Believed to be an enactment of the old regeneration theme (the Old King being sacrificed to make way for the Young King), traditionally, the tree of the wren is the ivy, while the robin is allocated the holly. As an example of trans-ference magic, the wren was expected to shoulder all the ills and problems of the people; effectively taking their bad luck, ill health, etc., leaving them free to hope for good health and prosperity in the coming year A simple rite preferable to the actual killing of a wren is as follows:

In the late afternoon before the Winter Solstice, visit your local wood *and ritually cut a length of flowering ivy, stating as you do so, that you are honouring the spirit of the Old Year. Wrap the ivy in a piece of silk and carry it home. Place the ivy in a central part of the house, where it can absorb all the dross accrued over the year — perhaps as part of the festive decorations. At dawn of Twelfth Night, re-wrap the ivy in its silk and return to the wood. Locate a strong **male** holly tree and wind the ivy round the base of the trunk, stating your intention. Offer thanks to the spirit of the ivy/wren, and then leave it to die.*

The intention of this ritual is to offer the life force of the old year in sacrifice, to the spirit of the new, so that it can flourish with extra vigour (as will your own fortune). Light a small fire and burn the silk (silk headscarves can be obtained quite cheaply from most charity shops). This represents the destroying aspect of the Goddess and by performing this rite, you will have enacted the entire birth-death-regenerative cycle. The reason why the traditional Midwinter 'hunting of the wren' now takes place in early January is because the shift from the Julian to the Gregorian calendar in 1582 that meant 11 days were lost in the process.

January evenings give us the opportunity to have a rare glimpse of flighting woodcock. The birds fly from the cover of the wood to the fields where they are feeding. They follow the rides in woods and the lee of high trees. Appearing at dusk, this bird is surrounded with magic and mystery; arriving with the first full moon after hard weather, they come across the North Sea from Scandinavia. A very handsome bird, they are considered a tremendously challenging sporting quarry as they fly very fast and not in a straight line. 'Roding' refers to the flight pattern of the male through woodland at dusk (designed to attract a mate), and takes place during early April when the males patrol the boundaries of their territory. A witch needing to employ magical diversionary tactics will find that rare woodcock feathers will enable them to 'rise silently and fly erratically' to avoid detection.

Toads, grass snakes and adders use the woods for hibernation and get out of the cold by squeezing into holes in the ground. Hedgehogs will have constructed impressive weatherproof nests in which they will sleep out the winter. Squirrels are much less active during cold spells and spend most of the day curled up in a drey, or nest; badgers sleep round the clock for several days in a row. It is during the bleak days of January when we are reminded that wild animals do not die peacefully of old age and that the culling, which takes place in the autumn does have a purpose in the natural scheme of things. As one old countryman commented: 'Nature offers wild animals three kinds of 'natural' death: disease, starvation or predation. Hunting and culling is predation regardless of the form it takes.'

The witch learns to interpret the language of Nature in all her guises. The telltale signs of footprints in snow and mud will tell you which animals and birds can be found in the vicinity. A five-toed, five-clawed imprint in the mud with a large bar-shaped pad shows that a badger passed this way on its nightly rounds and, although quite numerous, these tracks are often the only sign that a set is nearby. The old name for the badger is the *brock*, or *bawson* and those adopting it as a totem animal should accept that it is also a predator, digging young rabbits from their burrows. A rabbit's skin taken cleanly off and the carcass consumed; a rabbit's burrow with perpendicular hole dug down to it, or a wasp's nest cleaned out in the same way, all show a badger has been at work.

Similarly, a circle of feathers or a young bird lying with its body untouched but the flesh picked neatly from the neck and the head missing shows a sparrowhawk kill. Unless food is scarce, foxes rarely kill the rabbits near their den, and a dead rabbit with a small hole in its neck announces the presence of a stoat. A young pheasant without its head is an owl kill, while the same birds, with only the brain missing shows a jackdaw has been at work.

A snowfall in January is the best time to see and hear foxes. This is the height of the mating season, so we will hear the vixen's eerie scream and the dog-fox's answering call. Even for a witch used to the sounds of Hunter's Wood, it's enough to make your hair stand on end if the call is unexpectedly close. With the short days, foxes are more active and snow makes sure they are about far more in daylight hours. The cold weather makes them bolder, leading to attacks on livestock and pets — just like during the Wolf-moon of the Saxons. The telltale signs of a fox kill are the cleanly severed feathers (a raptor tears out the feathers of its prey); or a discarded hedgehog skin — a badger, which is the only other hedgehog-killer, does not leave the skin behind.

Although the smallest of predators, the weasel and stoat are by far the most courageous and either make an ideal witch's totem animal. Under extreme circumstances, when cornered or injured, a weasel will attack a man, displaying an inborn ability to strike directly at the human jugular. With its handsome chestnut-colour fur, the weasel can often be glimpsed hunting during the winter months despite the fact that it is less than 12 inches from tip to tail. A local name for the animal is *whittret*, or white throat, because of the white undersides. Besides man, the weasel's only predators are owls and hawks and it has been known to deliver a quick nip to the swooping bird's spine and thus the dinner becomes the diner. The stoat is larger and in the winter its coat turns white (ermine) but whether wearing its brown summer coat or winter white, it can be recognised by the black-tipped tail. And we must remember that predators like the fox, cat, stoat and weasel will kill to excess when the opportunity presents itself.

During February, Hunter's Wood presents a 'quiet spectacle of inactivity'. With the end of the pheasant shooting season the depleted stocks of cock pheasants that have taken sanctuary in the Wood strut and search for food in the leaf litter. There is, however, an increase of noise in the rookeries and on a fine day, these raucous birds can be seen indulging in aerobatics known in some parts of the country as 'shooting'. Discovering a thermal of warm air rising from the sun-warmed earth, the rooks are carried upwards with their wings outstretched. As the whole flock ascends, birds suddenly fall out of the sky, twisting and turning until they descent to treetop height. It has been suggested that this is connected to courtship and possibly an affirmation of their place in the colony.

Owls are known to everyone — even to those who have never seen or heard them — and it is the tawny owl that is essentially a woodland bird. It is seldom seen in open countryside, and can be found hunting as dusk is falling: a time between times often referred to by countrymen as *owl*-light. After dark, the tawny owl's characteristic hooting call has its own eerie quality — a haunting but strangely beautiful sound. There is an old saying that the owl is 'king of the night' but to the Romans, it was a symbol of death and feared for its supernatural powers. The bird's eerie cries enhanced the creature's supposed magical qualities and Roman superstition, readily accepted by the conquered tribes of Britain, perpetuated a hatred and fear of the bird. The Saxons knew the bird as *ūle* (named for its sad, lamenting cry), the word being corrupted to *oule* by medieval times. With an eerie silence descending over the winter wood and fields, the haunting cry of fox and owl is more easily heard. **And for the traditional witch these answering calls, when a magical working has been performed in the open, means that the spell has gone home.**

Just after the New Year, the winter aconite appears in sheltered spots in Hunter's Wood, opening in the weak winter sunshine and closing in dull weather. Also well established in parks and woodland, the plant is closely related to monkshood and, like its cousin, is highly poisonous. Bluebells leaves are beginning to push their spikes through the dead undergrowth as wild honeysuckle sends out its shoots in an attempt to gain a head start before the woodland canopy blots out the sunlight. In the damp places hidden away deep in the wood, the first thrusting spikes of primroses and snowdrops bravely push upward into the frosty air. During medieval times an ointment, made from primrose leaves boiled with lard was used by woodmen in the New Forest to treat cuts, while on May Day, bunches of primroses were laid on the floor of cowsheds to 'protect cattle from witches at a time when they were considered to be most active'!

In these bleak, grey days we can learn to use a poacher's trick that can act as a reminder of where to find a particular plant or nest. Pieces of broken white crockery remain visible however dark the night or dull the day, as they reflect any light there happens to be. Poachers would mark bushes, rabbit holes and *smeuses* used by hares to help them set nets, or when ferreting by night. The witch who works in the woods by night can employ this trick to help navigate the path to a sacred site without fear of losing the way.

For the traditional witch, woodland streams and pools are always points of enchantment, and there is nothing more evocative than the tinkle of water running over stones in the streambed. Fed by springs all year round, they now become rushing torrents swollen by rain and thawing snow. Winter debris of fallen leaves, twigs and branches dam the natural flow until the sheer volume of water breaks its banks, and runs unfettered across the woodland floor. The winter pool is ideal for scrying since this usually reflects the dark sky, overshadowed by the surrounding trees, and if we stare into the depths, we may see images in answer to the questions we need to resolve.

By February, however, the water recedes and on the banks of the stream, one of the most attractive and conspicuous of early spring flowers, the lesser celandine gleams golden in the weak sunlight. The gradual rise in temperature persuades frogs to leave the solitude of hibernation, and venture forth in search of stagnant water. Here, among the reed-lined water margins of the pool, they spawn. Frogs (and toads) have long been associated with witchcraft **and for the traditional witch the answering call of a toad or frog, when a magical working has been performed in the open, also means that the spell has gone home**. The immediate response of a fox (or dog), owl (or hawk) or frog (or toad) indicates that the witch is on her contacts at a higher level of Nature, even though these creatures may not necessarily be her or his totem fauna.

The Night Sky

If we decide it is safe to venture out into Hunter's Wood at this time of year, we will be greeted by cold clear nights that enable us to view the stars through the bare branches, just as our ancestors did thousands of years ago. November offers the opportunity to see two sets of annual meteor showers — the Taurids (25th October–25th November) and the Leonids (14–20th November) — and it is always advisable for a witch to wish upon a star.

From a dark country sky, we can see a dozen meteors or more an hour on any night of the year, depending on where the Earth is in its orbit around the Sun. For witches with an affinity to cosmic energies, the night of 3–4th January marks the peak of the major meteor shower — the Quadrantids. This is a good opportunity for stellar working in the direction of the constellation of Draco: Thuban, the brightest star in the formation was the Pole Star in ancient times. The best-known constellation in the northern hemisphere, however, is Ursa Major (the Great Bear) or the Plough with its seven stars. Opposite Ursa Major, although a very faint and distorted version, is Ursa Minor (the Little Bear) that contains Polaris, the modern Pole Star.

The distinctive grouping of Orion has crossed the celestial

equator and can be seen from every inhabited country. Orion is the Hunter, with his two brilliant stars, Betelgeux and Rigel, and his Belt and Sword, closely followed by Sirius, the Dog Star, (in line with the three stars of the Belt) and the brightest star in the heavens. It is the Hunter that dominates the night sky from now until the Spring Equinox — running in tandem with the traditional hunting season — magical workings for hunting down our own dreams and schemes are the order of the night.

Hunter's Wood is *very* old and nowhere will we feel more aware of this than standing beneath the bare trees in winter. Only now, in early-falling darkness of the short afternoon, do we become aware of the solitude; with dead leaves underfoot and the great, empty trees that no longer shut out the grey skies and the icy wind. How bleak the rooks' nests look, tossing against the grey sky as the light fades. This Wood is only hospitable in certain places and at certain times of the year, and it is good for us to be reminded of that sometimes; perhaps encouraging us to scatter some bread or dried fruit in offering before returning home out of the cold, and glad of a roaring ash-wood fire.

Spring Equinox

An old country saying: *I live too near a wood to be scared by an owl* — meaning 'don't try to frighten me with something familiar' and a witch should never fear an owl.

Astronomically taken to be the period from the Vernal Equinox to the Summer Solstice (occurring around 21st March and 21st June respectively in the northern hemisphere), spring is the time of birth and regeneration in the natural world. The word 'spring' is of Old English origin and has many other meanings; the Latin name for the season was *ver*, a word that is found in the adjective *vernal*, meaning 'of the spring'. It is the time when life returns to the countryside after the barren months of winter.

In Hunter's Wood the witch will find delicate wood

anemones, wood violets, dog's mercury and primroses braving the late flurries of snow. The leaves of the wood violet were once a delicacy, fried and eaten with sugar and lemon, while the leaves of the primrose were made into an ointment for wounds received in battle. Dog's mercury is called 'green waves' by some country people because of the sea-like motion as the leaves sway gently in the breeze. The whole plant is poisonous but the flowers were once used to make herbal enemas. Since it is not an attractive plant it is rarely picked so 'its harmful qualities are rarely given an opportunity to manifest themselves'. Wild daffodils, although becoming rarer, are still to be found in damp meadows and woods in England and Wales; and from late April until early June bluebells carpet the woodland floor.

Bluebells

> *Where the bluebells and the wind are,*
> *Fairies in a ring I spied,*
> *And I heard a little linnet*
> *Singing near beside*
>
> *Where the primroses and the dew are,*
> *Soon were sped the fairies all:*
> *Only now the green turf freshens,*
> *And the linnets call.*

Walter de la Mare

White swathes of wood anemones are found covering the woodland floor before the trees come into leaf. Also known as granny's nightcap and wind-flower, flowering from March to May. Like the winter aconite, the flowers droop in damp weather and at night to protect the pollen. This pretty little flower gives off a smell reminiscent of leaf mould and foxes and is often known by it's rural name of 'tod's weed'. The first anemone of the season was picked and sewed into the lining of a person's coat to ward off the evils of plague and pestilence; a witch can give the pressed flower to a friend, together with a wish for good health.

As an addition to the witch's kitchen, the strong smell of garlic in damp woodland means that ramsons are growing there. They have long-stalked shiny leaves like lily-of-the-valley, and heads of starry white flowers that appear from April to June. An ancient proverb says: *Eat leckes in lide* [March] *and ramsons in May/And all the year after physitians may play.* Also known as wild garlic, large colonies of ramsons can often be smelt yards away, and garlic woods sometimes count as landmarks in old land charters. The leaves can be used in salads and sauces as a substitute for garlic or spring onions.

In Hunter's Wood, the witch finds that trees respond quickly to the first hint of mildness and several flower long before they leaf, such as the alder, hazel and willow. The aspen tree also flowers in March before the leaves appear, bearing male and female catkins on separate trees. The catkins produce no scent or nectar, so will not be visited by any pollinating insects: pollination is carried out by the wind. The shape and size of the leaves vary according to whether they come from the main part of the tree or from the suckers. The leaves are copper-brown when they first break, turning to grey-green — usually paler on the underside, which gives the aspen its curious shimmering silver light. In the late autumn, the leaves turn to gold in a spectacular display. The leaves turn inwards, and one country superstition says that the leaves curl upwards when a thunderstorm is due.

To welcome the Spring Equinox (or Beltaine), collect a handful of flowers from the alder, hazel, willow, aspen and wych elm to create a 'woodland pot pourri' *of magical energies to act as a protective charm. This springtime collection represents new life/ideas and should be burned in the Beltaine hearth fire following a ritual to bring prosperity to your family and home.*

We also see that on the wych elm, the dense clusters of reddish-brown flowers begin to appear in March and April before the leaves, and note that the wych elm's flat fruit has the one seed in the centre of the fruit, not above the centre, as in the common elm. The flowers are brightly coloured with crimson or purple anthers and white filaments. The leaves are bright green; rough above and downy and rough on the underside. The wych can be also distinguished from the common elm by a number of characteristics. Wych elms are not as tall and grow in irregular shapes up to 100 feet. The lower branches start to arch from nearer the base of the trunk, while the upper branches appear twisted. The dull grey or blackish bark is smooth when young but turns brownish-grey, fissured and ribbed in mature specimens.

For the witch exploring the woodland, the following are three trees most easily spotted in the spring:

The dampness of the English spring doesn't stop the **alder** (*alnus glutinosa*), one of our most sacred of trees, from flowering during March and April. In Hunter's Wood these are found growing by the stream, by the woodland pool and on the marshy heathland. The little pink roots creep into the water from the bank — some actually growing in the water. It is a tall, fine-leaved tree with crooked branches; the whole trunk bending towards the water and often hanging over it.

Alder trees are usually found growing in clumps along the waterside — banks of rivers, lakes and marshes — but seldom on drier ground. The alder is able to thrive in marshy conditions because, unlike most other flora, its roots are able to form an association with bacteria that is capable of utilising nitrogen from the atmosphere. Alder trees put more nitrogen back into the soil than they use, so they build up fertility and alder swamps, when cleared and drained yield heavy crops. The fertile fens of East Anglia once supported many alder thickets.

The tree is easily identified by its black, fissured bark and in the winter, brownish-grey male catkins hand like lamb's tail from the tree. Male and female catkins grow in separate clusters on the ends of the tree's leafless twigs — the males opening in March and scattering golden pollen to fertilise the bud-like females, which develop into small green cones that turn brown in the autumn. The leaves of the alder are blunt with saw-like edges, and one-half of the leaf is rarely the same size as the other. When young the leaves are sticky and shiny above, with a fine whitish down in the angles of the prominent veins underneath. The tree does not produce any seeds until it has passed its twentieth year.

If you have an affinity with the alder (described as the 'Battle-witch of all Woods') then find what appears to be the oldest tree in the green wood and spend time familiarising yourself with its cycle throughout the seasons. Use the leaves, bark and catkins in your magical and path-workings, and its correspondences for spell casting and divination.

Fluffy yellow catkins on the **hazel** (*corylus avellana*) gives the sign that this is the first deciduous tree to come alive again from its winter sleep. In winter, the hazel can be identified by the small grey (male) catkins near the tips of the twigs. In early spring they expand to become pinkish-creamy yellow lambs' tails; at the same time the tree puts out tiny female catkins, like leaf-buds with red tassels. By late spring, the leaves have opened and in the autumn, the female flowers have ripened to form groups of two or three large brown nuts.

The hazel leaf is a dense, green colour that turns to brown and then yellow-gold in the autumn. The brownish-yellow catkins (lamb's tails) begin to develop in the autumn and burst into flower in the spring, dangling from the leafless twigs and releasing clouds of golden pollen. At least two hazel trees growing close together are needed for fertilisation and the production of nuts. This is because the female catkin usually ripens after the male flower of the same tree. The hazel can be seen as a harbinger of spring, displaying its cascades of golden flowers against the sombre backdrop of the wood. Beware of bringing sprays of catkins indoors as the falling pollen can mark furniture.

Hazel has always played an important role in rural life. It is good for pea sticks, bean poles, small stakes, or clothes props, and small straight spars and curved broaches or pegs used to secure thatch to the roofs of cottages or corn-ricks. Long shoots can be split to form hurdles. The wood makes first class kindling (traditionally popular for baker's ovens) and the rods used by water diviners are usually hazel.

If you have an affinity with the hazel (known in Celtic folklore as the 'Tree of Knowledge') then find what appears to be the oldest tree in the green wood and spend time familiarising yourself with its cycle throughout the seasons. Use the leaves, bark and nuts in your magical and path-workings, and its correspondences for spell casting and divination.

Willows are also well known for their attractive catkins — called 'pussy' willow. There are numerous species of in Britain but the most common are the white (*salix alba*) and crack (*salix fragilis*) willows. Both are found in damp woods, streams and woodland pools. The overall grey-whiteness of the white willow's foliage gives the tree its name. The long slender leaves with sharp-pointed tips are light green on top and covered with a thick down underneath, giving the leaves a silver sheen. The dark grey bark has a close network of deep fissures and ridges; the twigs are quite tough, in contrast to the crack willow, which has fragile twigs. The crack willow's leaves are narrow with coarsely toothed edges, and glossy green on top and bluish underneath.

If you have an affinity with the willow (known as the 'Tree of the Ancestors') then find what appears to be the oldest tree in the green wood and spend time familiarising yourself with its cycle throughout the seasons. Use the leaves, bark and catkins of the willow in your magical and path-workings, and its correspondences for spell casting and divination.

Listen to the gurgling sound of the stream that is always present in the wood, providing the background for spring and summer bird song. For the traditional witch, thoughts of death play little part in the emergence of spring. The woods are bursting into leaf; the dawn chorus gets louder and longer. Woodland birds are nest building, some are already sitting on eggs. Soon roe fawns will browse beside their mothers at dawn and dusk, while families of rabbits play in the shadows cast at sunset in the field margin at the edge of the wood.

Under the placid surface of the woodland pool, lies an aquatic 'jungle' teeming with a wide range of bacteria, insects, animals and plants. Woodland ponds are often too overshadowed to support much plant or animal life, and vegetation is normally restricted to algae and a few clumps of starwort. The bottom is choked with dead leaves, often covered with a tangle of dead twigs and branches but the murky depths of the spring pool also provide perfect conditions for scrying and divination. Here the colourful dragonfly emerges from the broken reeds. Dragonflies are among the fastest-flying and oldest insects in the world. Estimates of their speed vary from 35 to 60mph, and fossilised remains show that they existed 300 million years ago. While the kingfisher is never more than a flash of iridescent blue as it flies a few feet above a stream or pool.

Scrying in natural surroundings requires a still, reflective surface on the water, not a stream that is continuously flowing, and a woodland pool is ideal for this even if the water is slightly stagnant.

The pool will simulate water poured into a dark bowl in the comfort of the home but here in the wood we are susceptible to a different type of ambience. Staring into the dark water, we feel vulnerable and alone, and our scrying will generate completely different images to those experienced in the safety behind closed doors ... only repeated experimentation and experience will release us from this fear.

While the trees are still bare, it may be possible for us to catch sight of the small, unobtrusive tree creeper as it scurries up and down the tree bark searching for insects. Its quick, darting movements can be mistaken for a mouse as the brown and cream plumage blends against the bark. By contrast, the fast, vibrating drumming of the pied or spotted woodpecker can be heard from a considerable distance in the silence of the wood. This drumming is a form of 'song' used by the bird during courtship, to deter rivals and later to keep in contact with its mate. It is heard during the breeding season from January to June, and again in September.

For most witches, however, one of the first signs of spring is the sight of a bird carrying nesting material. The increased activity in the rookeries usually heralds the start of nest-building high in the treetops, where this jumble of twigs and mud lined with grass, wool and hair, remain at the mercy of any spring gales. The rook is a gregarious bird, often feeding and flying in large numbers and building up to forty nests in one tree. By contrast, the magpie constructs a veritable fortress of strong twigs and mud; its deep cup lined with fine roots and the dome a stockade of thorny twigs. Unlike their cousin, the rook, they will build in a thick hawthorn bush, which adds to the protection on the nest.

Black ants now begin to appear in the woods (red ants wait until the weather improves in April). Should you want the clean skeleton of a bird or small mammal for shamanic purposes, throw the body on the nest of wood-ants and 'it will be picked as clean and bare as if it had been scraped'. Often, jays, rooks, thrushes and starlings can be seen 'anting'. The birds deliberately crouch among a mass of ants, holding their wings out so the insects can crawl up into the feathers. There are 40 species of ants in Britain and most produce a toxic deterrent; it has been suggested that the birds use this 'insecticidal shampoo' to reduce the parasitic insects living among their feathers.

Night Sky

Spring is the start of a major 'change over' in the night sky. Orion is still on view during the early part of the night but by the end of the March, it will start to fade into the twilight. As spring approaches and the nights grow shorter, the witch should be aware of one of the most beautiful of all constellations — Virgo, named after its brightest star, Spica, and identified with Persephone, the goddess of spring — and the only female among the constellations of the zodiac and symbolises the fading of winter.

Also visible in the constellation is Gamma Virginis, or Porrima (named after the Roman goddess of prophecy) one of the most famous of 'double' stars. An excellent opportunity for divination and to see what the future holds in store. The Spring, or Vernal Equinox, falls around the 20–21st March which makes this an ideal time for building magically on what you wish to achieve in the coming months.

What we need to realise is that the population of every species is governed by the food ad habitat available. Nature's over generous birth rate creates an overgenerous death rate for the aging and sickly by saving the survivors from starvation and disease. A large number of pagans (who would be deeply hurt if labelled callous but who *are*, if unintentionally, just that), are unable to understand the absence of alternative to Nature's ways in Nature's world. Their revulsion at the 'taking of life' stops short of any consideration of what that life consists of when it ceases to meet the requirements that are demanded of those creatures of the wild that live it. Whatever we believe, or do not believe, the lives of free wild creatures will be lived *their* way, not ours.

Summer Solstice

In summer when the shaws be sheen
And leaves be large and long
Full merry it is in the fair forest
To hear the fowlés song.
16th century rhyme

Astronomically taken to be the period from the Summer Solstice to the Autumnal Equinox (occurring around 21st June and 23rd September respectively in the northern hemisphere), summer is the time of hot weather, ripening fruit and grain. The word summer is of Old English origin and invariably the time of year when temperatures are at their highest. The hottest days of the year are the 'Dog Days', a period of uncertain definition, but generally reckoned to last from 3rd July to 11th August. Associated with the rising of the Dog Star (Sirius) and according to ancient superstition, disease and disaster were rife at this time and dogs were at their most susceptible to rabies; in some towns and cities all dogs had to wear muzzles in public places for the duration.

One of the witch's favourite and most useful of trees comes into its own in summer. It is the only shrub that rabbits find inedible, and so it thrives on warrens and any soil rich in nitrogen from the animal dung and bird droppings. It can be found around badger sets, or forming shrubberies below tall trees used as roosts by starlings, pigeons and other birds. The tree gets its name from an Anglo-Saxon word meaning 'hollow tree', although it is often referred to as 'ellen', possibly from its associations with the Faere Folk. In June, the elder has spectacular clusters of creamy-white flowers with a heavy fruity fragrance, which are used to make elder tea and wine. By September, the branches are weighed down with bunches of juicy black berries for making wine and cordials.

A witch should also learn to recognise the woodland or Midland hawthorn, which is often found in the shrub layer of oak woods and can be distinguished from the common hawthorn by its leaves. The leaves are more rounded and broader than they are long. The tree flowers in May (hence its name), with the green berries beginning to turn red in August. In Hunter's Wood, these are unmolested by hedge-cutters and so these hawthorns can grow into substantial trees; in old age, the trunks become gnarled, twisted and furrowed. If we wish to collect material for magical working from the hawthorn, *this* is the tree we should choose.

As the deciduous wood spreads its canopy, a deep shade engulfs the woodland floor, and the flush of flowers that thrived in spring sunlight filtering through the bare branches begins to wane. The undergrowth has become choked with brambles, bracken, nettles and willowherb. The honeysuckle found at the edge of the wood is rooted six or ten feet back inside the trees because it knows that in dry late summer, the ground there will be damp and cool and the roots will be in the green shade. Along the woodland rides, blackberry flowers shine like stars against the deep glossy green of the leaves. The face of the surrounding countryside gradually changes from the fresh greens and bright colours of June, through the gold and brown of ripening crops and scorched grass in July and August to the early signs of the approach of autumn in September.

As we tread the woodland paths, we may find betony that has been treasured since ancient times as a remedy for many ills, especially for reducing fever. The Romans prescribed it for digestive troubles and liver complaints; the dried leaves being used as a substitute for tea, or powdered as a snuff. The plant grows in woods and poor grassland and bears bright maroon flowers from June to September. It may also be found in the ruins of ecclesiastical buildings where it was planted as a charm — hence its other name bishopswort.

Enchanter's nightshade's Latin name *Circaea lutetiana*, refers to the Homeric witch Circe, who turned Ulysses' crew into pigs. Its English name has similar magical connotations, but there are no dark properties attributed to it in English folklore. It grows in dark, shady places such as glades in woods — a tall, slender plant with spokes of small pink or white flowers, each with only two deeply notched petals from June to August. The nightshades would be perfect emblems of traditional witchcraft, particularly the woody nightshade, or bittersweet that is found in woods, hedgerows and waste ground, although the young stems were collected in autumn and dried for medicinal purposes, i.e rheumatism and skin complaints. In Lincolnshire, garlands were hung on pigs to protect them from malign influences. The purple plant flowers from June to September, developing into small red berries in the autumn.

Woody nightshade can be used for a 'Bittersweet Binding' against someone who is gossiping about, or slandering you. This binding is a method of 'staying a poisonous tongue' since woody nightshade or bittersweet is known to paralyse the central nervous system if taken internally. Here we use what is known as sympathetic magic, by binding the leaves or berries (both are toxic) of the plant, together with hair, nail clippings, saliva or a photograph of the guilty party. This preparation should be buried at the root of the woody nightshade with the demand that its poison shall still the gossiping tongue of your enemy.

Often overlooked by modern witches is the fact that among our woodland flora there are 1355 British species of lichen, of which

500 grow on shrubs and trees. The rest grow on walls, roofs, gravestones, rocks, chalk grasslands, heathlands and sand dunes. Lichens do not have roots but absorb water and gases through their upper surface, and are therefore sensitive to atmospheric pollution. Those on trees thrive best on the sunny, south-west aspects of trunks and branches, and the disappearance of lichen can be used to detect rising levels of air pollution.

> *Lichens have special healing and magical powers, and during medieval times were used in the treatment of a number of diseases. More recently, a number of substances found in lichens have been shown to have antibiotic properties that inhibit the growth of disease-causing organisms. Some lichens have been used in the treatment of various infections, and in ointments for wounds and burns, having been found to be more effective than penicillin. Magically, they provide us with a psychic 'cure-all' that can be used in charms and amulets of protection to ward off any ill-luck or negative energy.*

Strangely enough, although the winter woods are hauntingly beautiful and mysterious, it is the summer wood that can instil in us a feeling of panic, bordering on blind terror. It is in this world of dappled sunlight and shade that mysterious voices echo in shadowy glades and filmy apparitions glide on the periphery of our vision. There *is* an eerie feeling that we are not alone in this world of mysterious hidden things ... there *is* the sensation that from behind gnarled tree trunks watching eyes are following our every step. A feeling that intensifies as the sun sinks and the light fades ...

Nothing

Whsst, and away, and over the green,
Scampered a shape that never was seen.
It ran without sound, it ran without shadow,

Never a grass-blade in unmown meadow
Stooped at the thistledown fall of its foot.
I watched it vanish, yet saw it not –
A moment past, it has gazed at me;
Now nought but myself and the spindle tree.
A nothing! — Of air? Of earth? Of sun? –
From emptiness come, into vacancy gone! ...
Whsst, and away, and over the green,
Scampered a shape that never was seen.
  Walter de la Mare

Three trees that are at their most magnificent in the summer are the beech, lime and oak:

The **beech** (*fagus sylvatica*) is one of our handsomest of trees, and often believed to have provided the inspiration for Gothic archi-tecture but despite being a native tree; it plays little part in British folklore or traditional witchcraft. In summer, the heavy foliage prevents all but one-fifth of the sunlight from reaching the woodland floor, which is usually carpeted with a thick layer of fallen leaves and beech mast. For most of the year, the interior of the beech wood is dark, silent and still, just like the inside of a great cathedral. It is easily recognised by its smooth, grey bark, and slender zigzag twigs with pointed tips.

The winter twigs of the beech are very distinctive: slender, smooth and tipped with a spear-shaped bud, with each of the long, pointed buds is wrapped in a series of overlapping protective brown scales. The massive, smooth, silver-grey trunk makes this our tallest tree, and a well-grown beech grows to a height of about 100 feet, with a girth of 20 feet. The name beech comes from the Old English *bece*, and variations of the word survive in place-names such as Buckinghamshire, whose furniture industry was founded on the Chiltern beechwoods.

Beneath the tree, where the roots spread above the soil and the forest floor is covered with deep russet leaves, little can survive in its dense shadow. Our ancestors would have stuffed mattresses with dry beech leaves, which by all accounts, gave 'a comfortable, if noisy, night's sleep'. In France, they were called *lits de parliament* — talking beds — because of the noise they made. In the summer, the beech sports a dense overhead canopy that has a bright shining, almost translucent quality; but as the season advances, the leaves become stiffer and turn darker green with a glossy surface sheen. In autumn, the beech has few rivals as it glows with colour, displaying a brilliant patchwork of flaming orange, russet and gold.

If you have an affinity with the beech (which has been described as 'Mother of Forests') then find what appears to be the oldest tree in the green wood and spend time familiarising yourself with its cycle throughout the seasons. Use the leaves, bark and nuts in your magical and path-workings, and its correspondences for spell casting and divination.

The rare small-leafed **lime** (*tilia cordata*) is one of our oldest native trees, and what is known as the common lime (*tilia vulgaris*), is a hybrid of the large and small-leaved varieties. All limes have tall stems clad in smooth grey bark with vertical markings, and can grow to 80 or 90 feet high. The leaves are heart-shaped and the flowers, which are not produced until the boughs are well clothed with leaves, have a strong sweet fragrance of honeysuckle. The fruits are small and globular, with a characteristic fin to carry the fruits away from the parent tree on the autumn wind. This is one of our long-lived trees, with a life expectancy of some five centuries.

If you have an affinity with the lime (or 'Linden Tree' of poetic fame, takes its name from the Anglo-Saxon *lind*,) then find

what appears to be the oldest tree in the green wood and spend time familiarising yourself with its cycle throughout the seasons. Use the leaves, bark, fruits and flowers in your magical and path-workings, and its correspondences for spell-casting and divination.

English **oaks** can grow to 100 feet, may live for 800 years and make up one tenth of all English woods. The sturdy, massive trunk, the broad, rounded outline of its head, its wide spreading lower limbs are characteristics that cannot be confused with any other tree. The thick, rough bark is deeply furrowed in a large network pattern and the ground beneath the tree is littered with dried leaves and acorns. The tree may not come into leaf until mid-May and there may even be a second bursting of leaves known traditionally as the 'Lammas budding' since it tends to coincide with the Lammas festival on 1st August.

There are actually two native oaks in Britain, the **pedunculate** (*quercus robur*) and the **sessile** (*quercus petraea*), which can be told apart by the over-all shape of the tree and by the leaves. When growing in the open, the pedunculate oak is gnarled and tends to have lower, more horizontal and wide-spreading branches, so that the main trunk is hidden beneath a mass of boughs and leaves. The leaves themselves are pale green with two obvious 'ear-lobes' at the base, with deep indentations all round. The sessile oak has a straighter, less gnarled trunk, with branches growing from higher up. Its leaves are dark green, have no 'ear lobes' and the indentations are not so deep.

Oaks still account for one third of our hardwood trees, and this appears to have been the norm for the 60 centuries it has been established in the British Isles. The sentiment: *Hearts of oak are our ships* ... merely dates from the 18th century and refers to our sea-faring age between the Armada and Trafalgar when warships were made from this most durable and strongest of timber. Much of European mythology is based upon reverence of the oak and touching wood is an expression of this ancient cult, reflecting the belief that guardian spirits were present within the oak and must be appeased.

Of all British trees, the oak supports the widest variety of insect and other vertebrate life and more fungi are associated with it than with any other native tree. The tree has been likened to a crowded high rise block, inhabited at every level: birds and squirrels build nests in the crown, insects such as wasps, moths, beetles and weevils devour the leaves; ivy, mistletoe, lichens, mosses, algae and fungi invade the branches and bark; birds, insects and mammals feed on the acorns. 'Even the roots of the young oak are sought out by such insects as weevils and, as the oak lets in quite a lot of light through its leaves, flowering plants grow underneath it.' (*The Ever-changing Woodlands*)

If you have an affinity with the oak (described in 1662 by John Evelyn as the 'Wooden Walls' of England) then find what appears to be the oldest tree in the green wood and spend time familiarising yourself with its cycle throughout the seasons. Use the leaves, twigs, bark and acorns in your magical and path-workings, and its correspondences for spell casting and divination.

Although deciduous woodland may appear to be uninhabited, tucked away in the different layers of vegetation is a wide variety of our native fauna with which a witch may identify. From large deer, badgers and foxes to stoats, mice, shrews and voles, each with its own special niche within this rich environment. Competition for space is not as great as it is in the less complex habitat of fields or moorland, and many more species are accommodated into the woodland environment. Important factors are the height of the vegetation, the presence or absence of field or shrub layers, and whether there are areas of open land, scrub and old trees. Most animals are more dependent on the general structure of deciduous woodland rather than on any individual plant species.

By early summer, the male fallow deer is growing a new set of impressive and distinctive antlers in readiness for the autumn rutting season. This deer existed in Britain more than a million years ago, but died out during the Ice Age. Re-introduced by the Normans, its natural habitat is deciduous or mixed woodland with thick undergrowth. In the wild, fallow deer are shy and elusive and unless we move very quietly, they will take fright leaving us with just a fleeting glimpse as they run away.

The smaller roe deer can be found in most forested areas of Britain, and is as much at home in the sombre conifer plantations of the Scottish highlands as in the open hazel thickets of southern England. They have the ability to remain 'invisible', which has earned them the name of 'fairies of the woods'. A single thistle can be enough to break up the deer's outline and, once suspicious, the roe may stand motionless until quite certain that its presence has been discovered. Only then, will it bound away, displaying the characteristic patch of light coloured hair on its rump.

Beautiful but deadly

Whether we like to admit it or not, from an historical perspective, witchcraft and poison have been synonymous with each other. In reality, deaths from plant poisoning are extremely rare, although according to the Royal Society for the Prevention of Accidents, over 1500 people — mostly children — are taken to hospital each year with suspected wild-plant poisoning

All witches know that hemlock and deadly nightshade are deadly, but so are foxgloves, with high levels of a toxin called digoxin, which is used to treat heart conditions but which can be fatal in large doses. All parts of the plant are poisonous, and anyone with a heart complaint should avoid touching them, despite small doses of digitalis (prepared from the dried leaves) being used to treat certain heart ailments.

The same applies to two of our favourite wild flowers: daffodils and bluebells. Eating the bulbs of the former in mistake for onions can cause convulsions and paralysis due to the alkaloids in the roots. Bluebells contain glycosides, which can induce abdominal pain, diarrhoea and a slow, weak pulse if eaten, while the sap can cause dermatitis. While ragwort probably causes more animal loss than all other poisonous plants put together.

Monkshood or wolfsbane provided a powerful poison used to tip arrows for shooting game, and grows wild by shady streams in south-west England and South Wales ... as well as being sold in garden centres and florists! The beautiful, lush green carpet of dog's mercury can be just as deadly, as can the berries of the wild arum, commonly call 'lords and ladies' — and the elegant wild iris at the edge of the woodland pond.

Many plants and fungi found in British woodland *are* poisonous, and some are potentially lethal. There still remain many gaps in our knowledge of plant poisons and their effect, as there is generally no known antidote.

The Night Sky

As it is summer in the northern hemisphere, around the time of the full moon there is no real darkness in the night sky. This is because the sun never gets far below the horizon. Nevertheless, for the witch there are some interesting things happening in the heavens. The first star to appear is the brilliant blue-white Vega, in the constellation of Lyra, followed by Deneb (Cygnus) and Altair (Aquila); the three stars that form the Summer Triangle, which will remain with us until September. Stepping outside from a lighted room, your eyes will take some time to adapt and you will see very few stars. As your night vision settles down, more and more stars will be visible against the 'light' sky.

The nights are lengthening although the Summer Triangle continues to dominate the night sky, while the autumn constellation Pegasus makes its entry in mid-evening. The Pleiades rising from the east remind us that the hot days are over, and winter, with its frosts and fogs, lies ahead. August is the 'meteor month' with the Perseids peaking around 12th. This shower can always be relied upon to give a good display, and even around the full moon, quite a number of shooting stars can be expected. Gaze up into a clear, dark sky for a few minutes in the early hours of 12th and you will be very unlucky not to see several meteors.

Summer Solstice — the longest day on the 21st — is when the sun reaches its northernmost point in the sky. If we take precession and the various calendar realignments into account, this may be the original feast of Lammas/Lughnasadh — the feast of the sun and any celebration or working normally associated with the modern festival would quite easily transfer to the Summer Solstice. This can be looked upon as a time for bringing male energies to the fore. A good time to use solar energy in directing positive thoughts towards the coming winter months and any new undertakings.

Hunter's Wood, weather-beaten, hard-worked, interwoven with legend and history, stocked with its own exclusive selection of flora and fauna, is a traditional witch's 'life-raft from the past'. We do not need to spend very long amongst the mounds and stumps, and singular trackways to be persuaded that there may well have been a wood on this spot for thousands of years.

Autumn Equinox
Hazelnuts, conkers, blackberries, rose-hips and the early mountain-ash berries glowing in clusters bright as florescent beads. Old-man's beard climbing in grey-white sheets over

hawthorn and brambles along the edge of the wood. Beech leaves, chestnut leaves, oak leaves all colours, hanging still on a bright October afternoon; or pelting down-wind along the wet ground in a November storm.

Nature Through the Seasons, Richard Adams

Astronomically taken to be the period from the Autumnal Equinox to the Winter Solstice (occurring around 23rd September and 22nd December respectively in the northern hemisphere) the word comes from the Latin *autumnus*, and its use in English dates back to the 14th century. Although it is now the usual term for the season in the UK, in the USA 'fall' is preferred, although both autumn and fall were used synonymously in British English at one time. The latter appears in 16th century texts in the longer phrase 'fall of the leaf', but by the second half of the 17th century, the shorter 'fall' was certainly in use. The season of autumn carries with it certain negative associations of decay as it marks the transition into the barren months of winter, but for the traditional witch it is the most sacred time of the year.

Harvest is the culmination of the agricultural year and in the past, the very survival of a community hung upon its success. As a result, harvest celebrations have characterised the season of autumn throughout history. By the Middle Ages the celebration of the harvest was linked to the social hierarchy and economic realities of the emerging farming system in the form of the Harvest Supper, Harvest Home or Mell Supper. There were many different rituals to accompany the final act of harvesting with an element of local competition involved. In many areas the last sheaf was paraded in the form of a doll made from the corn, variously called a Kern Doll, Kern Baby or Harvest Queen. This observance has been revived in recent times in the craft of making Corn Dollies and a witch can embrace the spirit of the harvest celebrations by producing a simple corn plait tied with red ribbon, to hang by the hearth until next year.

Even in the deepest woodland it is important to pay homage to the bounty of the natural harvest on which wildlife will depend to survive the winter. Our hunter-gatherer ancestors also relied on the forest to provide warmth and shelter during the long winter months ahead. 'Flag, Flax, Fodder and Frigg' was a blessing used between traditional witches (Flag (or sometimes Fire) represents the hearth/home/warmth; flax is clothing; fodder is food (both animal and human) and frigg is sex), hoping the recipient has all these things in abundance. Here we take the opportunity to bestow our blessing on the woodland and leave token gifts to represent these four essential requirements for survival.

As well as the harvest of the grain, the picking of fruit in the orchards and vineyards, the witch will be gathering the natural harvest of wild fruit at this time of year. In days gone by much of the period after harvesting was taken up with the work involved in preparing food so that it would last through the lean months ahead. Many of the foods that we now enjoy as treats owe their origins in the life-or-death battle to survive the winter. Jams, pickles, smoked and salted meat and fish were all produced by processes that prevented foods from going off, allowing them to be stored for many months.

The rapidly approaching autumn inevitably draws the witch's thoughts to death and as the leaves fall from the trees, mild days bring colonies of different insects out onto the shiny foliage of the ivy. Wasps, bluebottles, winter moths, flies and drones (driven from the hive by worker bees) are tempted by the ivy's pale green flowers which bloom in late autumn. Wasps are by far the most abundant but these are the survivors of the summer population and will die as soon as the weather turns cold again.

The dark nights echo with the loud, shrill shriek of an owl as the bird searches for its prey. Often only seen as a ghostly shape in the half-light of dawn or dusk, it is not surprising that the owl is often the totem creature of witches. Owls enjoy basking in the weak sunshine and can sometimes be seen hunting on dull autumn afternoons. At night they patrol a clearly defined territory, cruising around 15 feet from the ground, listening for small birds and rodents in the undergrowth. The tips of the owl's wings are covered in fine down, which renders its flight almost silent — and added to its association with the world of magic and the supernatural.

Reminder: As any traditional witch will know, when performing a magical rite out of doors, the cry of an owl (or hawk), the bark of a fox (or dog), or the croak of a frog (or toad) in immediate response is a recognised sign that an invocation has been answered.

The first shades of autumn fall in the gentle month of September: sunny days with longer, cooler nights — then increasing wind and rain. With shorter days, and a weakening sun, the woodland can no longer sustain chlorophyll production and the trees begin to shut down. The decaying green pigment in the leaves is replaced by yellow and red ... each leaf stem is sealed off and the autumn winds do the rest. The woodland floor is now littered with a colourful carpet of fallen leaves, enhanced by brightly coloured fungi, while the autumn sunlight highlights the gold of the dying bracken.

The three trees to be easily identified in the autumn are the beautiful rowan (or mountain ash), the Scots pine and the yew. The **rowan** (*sorbus aucuparia*) has a straight, clean bole, clothed in smooth grey bark, scarred horizontally as though it had been scored with a knife. The twigs bear long feathery leaves, whose division into eleven to fifteen slender leaflets are similar to the ash, with tiny saw-like edges, which turn brown, red and yellow in the autumn. In the spring the delicate flowering branches bear a wealth of creamy-white blossom that develops into coral-red berries in late summer. The rowan loves moist soil, and although it can be found growing in both woods and gardens, it is common throughout the British Isles. In Scotland, the burns and lochs, and becks of the Lake District provide a spectacular backdrop for one of our favourite trees. It often grows singly, although in places there are naturally occurring pure rowan woods.

If you have an affinity with the rowan (also called 'Witch Wood' and 'Witchen') then find what appears to be the oldest tree in the green wood and spend time familiarising yourself with its cycle throughout the seasons. Use the leaves, twigs, bark, fruit and flowers in your magical and path-workings, and its correspondences for spell casting and divination.

The **Scots Pine** is recognisable by its pyramidal growth, although in old age the trees lose their elegant shape as the lower branches fall off and they become flat-topped and sometimes rather stricken-looking. The tree does best in peaty soil, but it thrives where there is sand, or even on a barren hillside, and it likes moisture. This is, of course an evergreen, and when the hills and woods are snow covered, the strong trunks and high branches with their dark green leaves stand out in relief against the wintry surroundings.

Sometimes we can see a clump of several trees growing together on top of a hill; they were thought to bring good luck, and the trees' imposing silhouette against the skyline made them an attractive focal point. All over the world the Scots pine is thought of in folklore as a symbol of fertility, longevity (it may live for a couple of centuries or more), and good fortune. There is also some evidence to suggest that single pines or small clumps, may well indicate the site of a ley line and particularly a 'node' point — a place where two or more ancient trackways intersect. This appears to be especially true if the trees are located on the top of a hill or mound, like those near Hunter's Wood.

Wordsworth extolled the virtue of the Scots pine, especially in the winter or by moonlight. And if you listen carefully beneath a cluster of pines when a gentle wind is blowing, you may hear secrets being told:

Stalwart and strong these sentry pines
Stand on the frontier line,
Guarding the gates to wonderland,
Whispering all the time.

If you would learn a simple lesson of the difference between a fir and a pine, remember that the leaves of the pine grow in pairs. They resemble two long green needles joined at the base. Search beneath a Scots pine and you should find several pairs of leaves that have fallen. These pairs of long leaves grow in circles, close together, so that the twigs look like bottle-brushes, whereas the firs have shorter, less bunchy-looking leaves. Pine cones do *not* forecast weather as is popularly supposed. They open and close as the weather changes from dry to wet, not in advance of the change. The cones open when it is dry so that the wind-borne seeds have a chance to scatter. Were they to open during wet weather, the rain would carry the waterlogged seeds straight down to the tree's roots.

If you have an affinity with the Scots pine (known world-wide as a symbol of longevity and good luck)) then find what appears to be the oldest one near the green wood and spend time familiarising yourself with its cycle throughout the seasons. Use the leaves, twigs, bark and cones in your magical and path-workings, and its correspondences for spell casting and divination.

The **yew** is a dark, brooding, evergreen that reaches a height of fifteen to fifty feet; the trunk is massive because of the numerous shoots joining together. The shade beneath a large yew is extremely dense, which means that not enough sunlight filters through to allow any green plants to grow, although Percival Westell thought it: 'A beautiful tree in winter or early spring, when small scarlet fairy lamps hang about its dark green cloak.'

The long flat leaves are poisonous and so are the seeds and bark — the crushed seeds were once used as an arrow poison. The small male flowers appear in clusters but the female flowers are solitary. These develop into a hard olive-green seed inside a red fleshy cup, which birds enjoy as they are sweet and full of syrup. In medieval times, the resin was used in ointments and plasters for wounds, skin irritations, and the oil added to bathwater was supposed to relieve muscular aches and pains. The ground inner bark of the tree was used to make bread, or mixed with oats to make griddle- cakes; the cones were used to flavour beer and wine.

If you have an affinity with the yew (known as both sacred and deadly) then find what appears to be the oldest tree in the green wood and spend time familiarising yourself with its cycle throughout the seasons. Use the leaves, bark and seeds in your magical and path-workings, and its correspondences for spell casting and divination but beware of its poisonous qualities.

Hunter's Wood in autumn has a beauty all of its own, but hidden away at the foot of the trees are other dangers that are not always beautiful. By the end of September, the hedgerows and woods will be displaying an impressive collection of wild fungi right through into October. There are some 3,000 species, of which about 50 are edible but even if you don't fancy eating them, these strange variants provide interesting colour and texture to the autumn tapestry. There's lots of folklore and Craft-lore pertaining to the identification of wild mushrooms from being able to peel edible ones or poisonous ones turning blue when touched with a penny (a pre-decimal penny, that is) but the best advice of all is to leave well alone if you don't know what you're looking for. Invest in a reliable guide and be safe rather than sorry but pictures may not always be reliable.

The four most lethal are the **Death Cap** (*amanita phalloides*) found in deciduous woodland, mainly under oak and beech; developing a distinct sweet, honey smell when fresh, or an unpleasant ammonia smell when old. The death cap grows in deciduous woods, particularly beech and oak, appearing in late summer and autumn is responsible for more than 90% of human deaths from fungus poisoning. Although sometimes mistaken for a mushroom, it has a pale olive-yellow cap and white gills. Once eaten, intense stomach pains start a few hours later, followed by paralysis. There is no known antidote, although a serum produced from a rabbit's brain and stomach was once believed to relieve patients! Regarded as the most poisonous fungi in the world, it appears during summer and autumn on woodland floors.

Destroying Angel (*amanita virosa*) also has a sweet, honey smell. It contains a lethal slow-acting poison and is believed to have killed the Roman Emperor Claudius. Although rare, it is found occasionally in broadleaved woodland in the autumn, but more commonly in coniferous forests. It has a white, rather sticky conical cap with white gills, and is supported on a slender white stem.

Panther Cap (*amanita pantherina*) although rare, is found in both coniferous and deciduous woodland (especially beech), in the autumn. The cap is smoky-brown with pale flecks but has no distinctive smell.

Fly agaric (*amanita muscaria*) with its distinctive red and white cap is usually found from August to November, particularly in coniferous forests. It causes violent intoxication and sickness if eaten, and the Vikings are believed to have eaten small amounts before going into battle. It is possibly one of the most beautiful of the species and a firm favourite of illustrators of fairy tales, but only deadly if eaten in large quantities. It gets its name from the traditional household use of mashing it with milk and sugar to use as bait to kill flies.

All these fungi are highly toxic and can kill. Or as one countryman said: 'Eat half a Death Cap and it's not a case of whether you may die, but how long it will take you to die.'

With all this violent energy around it explains why the natural tides around the Autumn Equinox are often chaotic and unsettled. This is obviously a time for male magical workings, particularly around the time of the Autumn Equinox on the 21–22nd but do not be tempted to use any fungi in magical preparations if you are not 100% sure of what you are dealing with.

To observe the Autumn Equinox and the traditional descent into winter requires the harnessing of male or Horned God energies. Each year there is the myth enactment of the Goddess (Nature) slipping into death or hibernation, while the God (or Holly King) watches over her while she sleeps until spring. This symbiotic relationship can be represented by the feathers of a wood pigeon (silver) and a cock pheasant (gold). To re-affirm the faith of the witch, collect four feathers from each bird from the woods and field margin where they roost and preen. Bind the feathers together to symbolise the continuity of natural cycles and tides changing from light to dark, day to night, summer to winter, and of regeneration and rebirth. Tie the bunch to the branch of your totem tree in the deepest part of the wood, and re-affirm your belief in the Old Ways and the power of the Ancestors. Leave a suitable offering on the ground below to be taken by the wildlife.

As the month draws to a close we see the last remaining leaves fall from the trees in a last burst of glorious colour. The dead leaves now form a thick carpet of brown and gold, and crackle underfoot as we attempt to move stealthily through the woods. Spectacular storm clouds of purple and grey accompany driving rain and winds, while branches are ripped from the host trees and brought crashing down to the woodland floor ... and in the eerie quietness that follows, we can think about an extract from the Thomas Hood poem, *Autumn*:

> *I saw old Autumn in the misty morn;*
> *Standing shadowless like Silence, listening*
> *to silence, for no lonely bird would sing*
> *Into his hollow ear from woods forlorn,*
> *Nor lowly hedge nor solitary thorn; —*

By late November, only the evergreens remain in leaf to add colour to the landscape although there are only three native species — the yew, the juniper and the Scots pine or fir. Standing on the edge of Hunter's Wood and looking out across the empty field, the stand of Scots pine on the distant mound appear as strange shapes rising out of the mist. Pollen records show that the Scots pine was the first tree to reappear when the Ice Age ended and at this time of the year, it bears two types of cones. One is the tiny, pea-like cone that is in its first year, and the larger, tapering cones that will turn brown in the spring to release the papery, winged seeds. Fallen cones can be collected to add to *pot pourri* and Yule decorations, or to be burned on the fire to release a pine fragrance into the room.

The Night Sky

The arrival of Orion, the Hunter, rising on the eastern horizon is heralded by the Orionid meteor showers that appear between the 20–22nd October. These originate close to the eastern horizon, near Betelgeuse. Orion rises in the east very late in the evening and well before that some of the members of the Hunter's retinue are well in view — Capella, Aldebaran and the Pleides. The Summer Triangle can still be seen for a while longer and will not start to disappear until late in October. From the magical perspective, this is an ideal time to welcome the Lord of the Wild Hunt as he prepares to take centre stage from now until the spring when he returns to the southern hemisphere.

The gurgle of the woodland stream now battles against the voice of the wind, and in autumn and winter it often drowned out by stormy days, when the wind roars through the wood sounding more like the mighty seas. Trees buffeted by the gales creak and groan like souls in distress but there is a wildness here that a traditional witch will find exhilarating.

Chapter Five

Guided meditations and pathworking

A Winter's Tale

This exercise can be performed at home or outdoors. For home-working, we begin with a visualisation and set the scene with the use of candles and some form of woodland contact, such as a bowl of leaves, a piece of bark, or vase of twigs. By using the imagination, we set the scene in our mind of a winter wood-scape with snow drifting between the trees. The sky overhead is a dull steel grey, with the promise of more snow to come. There is an unseen path that we instinctively follow through the wood until we come to a fallen tree ...

If working outdoors, it would be appropriate to try the exercise when confronted by an actual casualty of the winter winds.

Go into the woods after a violent winter storm and we will often find some veritable giant has been felled by the gales. A brooding sky, visible through the bare branches, is filled with more snow and all around the trees stand motionless, shrouded in an icy mist. Now some familiar tree lies where once only its dense shadow fell, great branches split and shattered; the bark with its multiple scarring, and the roots ripped from the earth, clawing towards the sky as though in supplication.

This tree in life was the very embodiment of the eternal force of Nature, a monument to strength and resilience but now it lies on the ground, an equally poignant testament to that same relentless force. The result of so many years' growth and struggle, this tree is now victim of the wind and snow. Although we feel sad at its passing, it doesn't seem appropriate to walk on without some form of acknowledgement. So, we take the time to sit awhile to ponder, and pay our respects to this fallen warrior.

Sad thoughts slowly subside as hope rises. In mourning the demise of this ancient tree, along with the sadness at its passing is the knowledge that new life will follow. Where once nothing grew because of the dense shade there is now light and hope. As the tiny seed, out of which grew this noble tree, found earth in which take root and light to grow towards, so too will other seeds find all they need in this patch of the now vacant forest floor.

Use this exercise as a basis for meditation, or set the scene and then allow your mind to wander where it will into a full pathworking. At the end of the exercise, clap your hands to earth yourself and have a couple of sweet biscuits and a hot drink close by. Even out in the woods, this is the best method of clearing any psychic dross from hanging about.

Spring

This exercise can be performed at home or outdoors. For home-working, we begin with a visualisation and set the scene with the use of candles and some form of woodland contact, such as a bowl of leaves, a piece of bark, or vase of spring flowers. By using the imagination, we set the scene in our mind of a spring landscape with a gentle rain filtering through the pale green veil of new leaves. The weak spring sunlight appears between the showers, leaving the wood glistening with iridescent raindrops. There is an unseen path that we follow instinctively through the wood until we come to a large sheltering oak ...

If working outdoors, it would be appropriate to try the exercise when able to sit beneath an old oak tree ...

We sit beneath the oak sheltering from a spring shower. Above the trees, the grey clouds with their promise of more rain move slowly, dampening and dulling the land.

Shifting patterns of shade and light move through the woods and with each cloud's passing comes a dream-like brilliance. The new leaves, wet with rain, shimmer in the weak sunlight, while a gossamer veil of minute droplets floats through the trees.

Safe and dry in the shelter of the mighty oak, we are deep within the woodland's fold — within the sphere of this oak's green leaf-light. The spring breeze draws another cloud over the wood and more raindrops patter on the oak leaves. Here we are part of the natural cycle of Life where trees are a bridge between the Earth and the sky, and in their leaves the four Elements meet.

Here **Water** floats in **Air**. Carried by the breeze to where it is needed. The broad, spreading branches of the oak lift the leaves up to the sky to capture the light, and soften the rainfall. Leaves draw up water from the roots deep within the **Earth**; the breeze stirs the leaves. Using the energy of the sun (**Fire**), leaves turn in the wind and rain; as they do carbon dioxide is absorbed into the tree and oxygen released into the atmosphere. Just as drops of rain combine to make great oceans, down here in the leaf-light, the ferns and enchanter's nightshade harvest the light and moisture left by the trees.

Use this exercise as a basis for meditation, or set the scene and then allow your mind to wander where it will into a full pathworking. At the end of the exercise, clap your hands to earth yourself and have a couple of sweet biscuits and a hot drink close by. Even out in the woods, this is the best method of clearing any psychic dross from hanging about.

Those Summer Nights

This exercise can be performed at home or outdoors. For home-working, we begin with a visualisation and set the scene with the use of candles and some form of woodland contact, such as a bowl of leaves or a piece of bark. By using the imagination, we set the scene in our mind of a summer evening landscape with a gentle red light from the setting sun filtering between the trees. In the quietness of the wood, there is the sound of running water from the stream and bird song hovering on the breeze. There is an unseen path that we follow instinctively through the wood until we come to a large clearing ...

If working outdoors, it would be appropriate to try the exercise when able to find a peaceful spot.

Before we begin this exercise, let's reflect for a moment on the following extract from Walter de la Mare's *Dream Song*, which will help to set the mood, especially if using the first two-line refrain as a chant while meditating.

Sunlight, moonlight,
Twilight, starlight –
Gloaming at the close of day,
And an owl calling
Cool dews falling
In a wood of oak and may.

Lantern-light, taper-light,
Torch-light, no-light
Darkness at the shut of day.

Elf-light, bat-light,
Touchwood-light and toad-light
In wild waste places far away

As dusk begins to fall in the wood, trees are silhouetted against the last rays of the dying sun. This is the time when the predatory animals of the forest begin to stir. The night air is perfumed with the smell of honeysuckle and as the darkness deepens the eerie blue-green glow of the honey fungus on decaying tree trunks, illuminates our path through the wood. These 'fairy sparks', believed to be the lights prepared for fairies at their revels, are caused by a natural phosphoric light from decaying wood.

In this strange half-light ... this time between times ... even the most familiar woodland is transformed into a supernatural dream-scape of the imagination. We can understand why our ancestors viewed the forest with a large degree of fear, tempered with a mystery that was intensified by the deep shadows hidden within its depths. From where we stand, these mythological and enchanted places are still full of magic and witchcraft, and peopled with strange beings.

Here and now ... at *owl-light* ... mysterious voices echo in shadowy glades and filmy apparitions glide on the periphery of our vision. We have the very real feeling that we are not alone ... that these things are not imagined, and no longer hidden from us. Again, there comes the sensation that gnarled tree trunks conceal watchers that are following our every step. That feeling intensifies as the sun sinks and the light fades ... and as the shadows deepen we begin to see faces in the bark of the trees.

Fear prickles along our spine and the hairs on the back of our neck stand on end, but a secret pathway is opening up and calling us ... we can't turn back although there is an impenetrable barrier of waist high brambles, nettles and bracken. We *must* follow the path through deeper undergrowth to find where it will lead ...

Use this exercise as a basis for meditation, or set the scene and then allow your mind to wander where it will into a full pathworking. At the end of the exercise, clap your hands to earth yourself and have a couple of sweet biscuits and a hot drink close by. Even out in the woods, this is the best method of clearing any psychic dross from hanging about.

Autumn

This exercise can be performed at home or outdoors. For home-working, we begin with a visualisation and set the scene with the use of candles and some form of woodland contact, such as a bowl of dried leaves, a piece of bark or incense made from pine cones. By using the imagination, we set the scene in our mind of an autumn afternoon walk in the woods, with dry leaves crackling beneath our feet. There is a cold nip in the air but the pale winter sun casts a shimmering golden veil between the boughs above our head. There is an unseen path that we follow instinctively through the wood until we come to a open glade fringed with dying bracken …

If working outdoors, it would be appropriate to try the exercise when able to find a similar spot.

Most of the leaves have fallen from the trees and lie in deep drifts on the woodland floor. We enjoy the almost childish delight of kicking them around and listening to the crackle as we walk deeper into the wood. The late afternoon is warm and sunny and we have a clear view through the trees, although there is now a filmy blue veil of wood smoke hovering in the still air. We feel at peace with ourselves …

Suddenly we become aware of a change in atmosphere. Nothing around us has changed but there is a feeling that something unexpected is about to happen. We stop our noisy game and start to walk more stealthily between the trees; we are stalking *something*, but we don't know what it is. The early autumn frost has flattened most of the undergrowth, but there are many huge clumps of bracken in which we can conceal ourselves and wait. We have stepped into the shoes of our hunter-gatherer ancestor …

Then we see him. A magnificent fallow buck emerges from the smoke haze, his dappled coat providing perfect camouflage against the autumn tones of the wood. These are the deer that would have lived alongside our ancestors. The buck's acute sight and sensitive hearing will alert him to any hint of danger and so we remain still and silent in our den of bracken. We admire his graceful curving neck and magnificent antlers with the broad, flat palms that distinguish these deer from other native species.

His brown eyes are set in the side of his head to give wide-angled vision, large ears that can be swivelled in the direction of the slightest sound. Then, he sees us ... but instead of taking fright, he simply stares back. The eyes change from deep pools of liquid brown to human in appearance and, almost superimposed over the shape of his head like the double-exposure of a photograph, there is another, more fleeting image. We suddenly recall that passage from a childhood favourite, *Wind in the Willows* where Mole and Rat encounter the Vision. 'Afraid! Of Him? Oh, never, never! And yet — and yet, I am afraid!' There is a flash of sunlight between the trees and the Vision vanishes. And we know exactly how they felt.

Use this exercise as a basis for meditation, or set the scene and then allow your mind to wander where it will into a full pathworking. At the end of the exercise, clap your hands to earth yourself and have a couple of sweet biscuits and a hot drink close by. Even out in the woods, this is the best method of clearing any psychic dross from hanging about.

Chapter Six

The Evergreen World

Before me rose an avenue
Of tall and sombrous pines;
Abroad their fan-like branches grew,
And, where the sunshine darted through,
Spread a vapour soft and blue,
On long and sloping lines
'Prelude', Henry Wordsworth Longfellow

For the witch, the tempo of life in an evergreen wood is quite different, both in the physical and the astral world. And although about half of Britain's woodland consists of conifers, as we know, only three species of tree are native to the country: the Scots pine, yew and juniper. All the other types have been introduced, firstly for ornamental purposes and then for timber production. Apart from a few remnants of the native Caledonian pine forest of the Scottish Highlands, the other coniferous areas have been planted within the last 50 years.

Nevertheless, pinewoods are a common sight in many parts of Britain and Europe and what we recognise as the Scots pine, grows as a native species in more countries than any other conifer. It extends from the Atlantic to the Pacific and from the Arctic to southern Spain, so some witches may be more familiar with the evergreen world, than broadleaved woods. In these *new* plantations, however, the trees grow in straight rows, and are all roughly the same age! The conifers stand close together, their branches meeting to form a canopy so dense that no flowering plants can grow beneath them. Instead, the woodland floor is a bare, soft layer of brown needles but here there is still magic to be wrought and magical materials to be found.

The actual appearance of an evergreen such as the Scots pine does not change much from one season to another, but the actual shape of the tree itself alters dramatically as it matures, depending on the habitat it lives in. A young Scots pine, for example, has a typical broad, conical shape with upturned branches; a mature tree in an open habitat develops the characteristic flat-topped crown that makes it so instantly recognisable. In the confined space of a forestry plantation, a Scots pine takes on a very different shape: much more upright and narrow, with a more pointed crown. Nevertheless, it is still the same Scots pine as that growing on the mound by Hunter's Wood, and it still has the same magical propensities.

Until the Middle Ages much of the Scottish Highlands were covered with forests of Scots pine. From the 17th century onwards, deforestation took its toll and today the native pinewoods of Scotland survive only as pathetic remnants. To see the trees at their best we must go to places such as Glen Affric in Inverness-shire, the Ballochbuie district of Aberdeenshire or Rothiemurchus on the north-eastern slopes of the Cairngorms. These genuinely wild pine forests, where pines of all ages and sizes grow amid majestic scenery of mountains and lochs, support a rich variety of flora and fauna. Here the trees grow in patches of different ages and sizes, sometimes including veterans up to 300 years old. The trees themselves are varied in form, from the usual conifer shape with slanting branches to those with widely spreading crowns. Some are grouped closely; other are spaced between open, sunny glades where we will find bilberry, juniper and heather on the forest floor.

The **juniper** (*juniperus communis*) is a rigid bush, its branches densely packed with narrow needle-like leaves. Each leaf is about ¾ inch long; the upper surface has a waxy blue-green sheen, with the underside being a much darker grey-green. The leaves taper to a stiff point that makes them prickly to touch. The juniper resembles a miniature yew, and sometimes they grow together — in Wales, it is known as the dwarf yew. The juniper 'flowers' in May or June and in the autumn the female cone forms a hard green berry that remains on the bush for two or three years before ripening into fleshy berries. The berries are blue-black in colour covered in a greyish bloom. The poet Laurence Binyon described the juniper:

> *The slope is darkly sprinkled*
> *With ancient junipers.*
> *Each small secret tree:*
> *There not a branch stirs.*

Juniper sticks were burnt on the hearth fire to scent rooms with their aromatic fragrance; elsewhere in Europe this was done to keep evil spirits at bay and protect the house from sorcery. Sprigs were hung above doorways on the eve of May Day to keep away evil, and burnt at Hallowe'en (Samhain) to ward off evil spirits. For magical use, juniper oil can be bought from chemists, while dried juniper berries can be found in any good supermarket.

If you have an affinity with the juniper (described by Culpeper as 'a solar shrub') then find what appears to be the oldest tree in the wood and spend time familiarising yourself with its cycle throughout the seasons. Use the leaves, bark and berries in your magical and path-workings, and its correspondences for spell casting and divination.

And yet the more familiar conifer plantations should not always be viewed as dark, soul-less rows of silent trees, and where the canopy is lighter, ferns will grown on the forest floor. In well-managed forests — from the newly planted to the mature — there is also a 'patchwork of mini-habitats' in which a variety of wildlife finds a home. Although some are so densely planted that they blot out sound and light, in the permanent twilight of the evergreen canopy we are reminded of the writings of those Romans who encountered the fierce Northern tribes and the dense forests that gave them protection. Or like the magical passage from John Fowles' *The Magus*:

> *It was a place where nature was triumphant over man. Not savagely triumphant ... but calmly, nobly triumphant. Man was nothing in it. It was not so bleak that he could not survive in it — but so vast that he could not equal or tame it. Above all, there were the silences. The evenings. Such peace. Sounds like a splash in the lake, or the scream of an osprey, came across miles with a clarity that was incredible — and then mysterious because, like a cry in an empty house, it seemed to make the silence, the peace, more intense. Almost as if sounds were there to distinguish the silence, and not the reverse ...stretching out to infinity, through the forest, over the water, into the stars.*

The witch can generally discover conifer woodland on uplands, where trees once grew before intense sheep grazing prevented natural tree regeneration. Forestry planting can also be found in sheltered valleys and lowland sites where the conifers are often mixed with deciduous hardwood trees of oak or beech, where the rides and firebreaks function like hedgerows and lanes. Although once the canopy layer is established there is no under-growth, the edges of the more permanent ride are quickly colonised by grasses, bracken and flowers. Here we can find our ingredients for spell casting and divination.

This 'artificial' woodland still offers much needed shelter in winter for a variety of animals; so much so that the increasing acreage of conifer plantations has encouraged the spread of animals such as the red deer that was once confined to the relic pinewoods of Scotland. Here we may also find different totem animals native to the conifer forests, including the wildcat, pine marten and red squirrel.

The true 'night-owl' is the long-eared owl and the difficulty in seeing them can be explained in three words: darkness, camouflage and silence. It occupies woodland, including conifers, roosting by day in branches close to the tree trunk. Sparrowhawks and buzzards are common predatory birds of conifer woods, although the buzzard is a bird of upland valleys, moorlands and woodlands, frequently nesting in conifers, building close to the main trunk of the tree.

As we have already seen, all living creatures can act as omen bearers and from a traditional witch's point of view, the materialisation of our dark forest 'totem' will tell us that we are on our magical contacts.

Pine cone magic

As well as being a food source for birds and animals, conifer seeds have long been an important part of our ancestor's diet. The Romans used to eat the seeds of the stone pine and introduced the species to Britain for that purpose. Cones have also been a source of fuel and for dyeing; not to mention the evergreen decorations for the Midwinter festival.

If working with the dark forest energies of the pinewoods, cones from conifer trees can become useful magical tools. This natural material is multi-purpose: it can be chopped fine for incense; utilised as a meditational tool in providing the smell of the pine woods; used an ingredient in spell-casting; as part of an altar garland and, for an added bit of psycho-drama, buy some of those wonderful copper sulphate-coated pine cones that produce the most amazing coloured flames. Or place a huge wooden bowl filled with different types of cone in the living area as a decorative feature.

Spell for good fortune:

A spell for good fortune is about a general improvement in circumstances rather than drawing wealth. Remember that *you can't change anything but yourself, but in changing yourself, everything changes around you*. Magical workings are influenced by the amount of effort we put into them, but if we are content to rely totally on coloured candles and the 'right' incense' to make the changes, then the results might be a long time acomin'.

- In the quest for good fortune, go for a divinatory or meditational result. The pine is a universal symbol of longevity and good fortune, so use the seeds from the cone to magically sow for *ideas to germinate*.

- Take twelve seeds from a selection of pinecones to represent each month of the coming year. Carefully fold them into a clean piece of paper or small envelope and write your wishes for the good fortune that you hope is to follow. Pass the written words through incense smoke made from dried pine, repeating your request aloud. Empty the twelve seeds into the palm of your hand and burn the words in the incense container.

- Being careful not to drop any of the seeds, take them to a spot where they can be scattered and allowed to grow. Breathe the 'breath of life' into the seeds and throw them into the protection of a hedgerow, or waste ground where they will not be disturbed — repeating your request aloud. Even if the seeds do not germinate, you will have supplied food for wildlife.

- Now wait for the 'signs' to manifest to suggest the changes you might make to your life to bring about your change of fortune. Receive and meditate on each sign as it comes, no matter how insignificant, and the answer will be revealed.

Window on the past

Conifers produce a sticky, transparent resin when any part of the tree is damaged — a defence system that has been in operation for at least 70 million years! The resin eventually becomes buried and fossilised into lumps of amber, frequently encapsulating perfectly preserved insects and plant remains. Amber was one of the first substances used to make jewellery and has long been recognised as material for a witch's amulet, if not a badge of 'rank' in some traditions.

A piece of amber or jet (fossilised wood) jewellery is a more subtle statement than the standard pentagram pendants, and provides a far older link with our distant ancestors. These are the 'gems' of the ancient forests and can often provide instant psychic links for divination and meditation purposes.

Amber: Amber was worn as jewellery, or carried as a talisman against injury on both the physical and astral planes. Helps disperse negative energy and speeds self-healing. In medieval times, it was believed to reveal the presence of poison.

Jet: Jewellery made from jet has been found at many ancient burial sites and provides a special link to the Ancestors. It has long been worn as a protective amulet and its powers help increase psychic and divinatory abilities.

Because amber and jet are the ancient by-products of the forest, it stands to sense that a 'wood-witch' would probably have a greater empathy with these than other gems and crystals. Try to obtain a piece of each and, once cleansed of outside influences, try including them one at a time in your magical workings to see if they improve your psychic powers. Both are now becoming rare and expensive, so beware of the synthetic variety that is now passed off as the genuine thing in many shops.

Pathworking: The Path Through the Forest

Our first attempts a pathworking into the evergreen world may make us feel uncomfortable, but a traditional witch needs to develop the ability to interact with Otherworld — and this is an easy way to take those first steps using music to create the psycho-drama often needed for successful magic.

Darwin commented that he believed the power of producing and appreciating music existed among the human race long before the power of speech. Perhaps that is why we are so subtly influenced by it, because there are vague memories in our universal subconscious of those misty times when the world was in its infancy. To set the scene for this pathworking an ideal piece of music is the *Pines of Rome,* a symphonic poem written in 1924 by the Italian composer Ottorino Respighi. Each movement depicts pine trees in different locations in Rome at different times of day.

The first movement, *I pini di Villa Borghese,* portrays children playing in the pine grove in a garden but it provides a relaxing two and a half minutes before the drama starts. The second movement, *Pini presso una catacomba* is a 'majestic dirge', representing pine trees near a catacomb and suggesting the subterranean nature of the catacombs, with the use of trombones to represent priests chanting. This is an ideal piece of dark, sombre music that is only seven minutes long but it is evocative of the eerie nature of the realms of Otherworld. Play the piece through a few times before attempting the pathworking, and so avoid any surprises in the tempo.

Start by visualising row upon row of tall, straight pines, stretching away from you in all directions, with nothing in between but ribbons of mist, swirling between the trunks of the trees like wood smoke. The overhead canopy obscures the light, and everything on either side is shadow and silence; there is a strange yellowish glow ahead … as if the sun is trying to break through the gloom. You walk forward along the open ride towards the glow, with only a ribbon of dying bracken separating you from the dense forest on either side …

The third movement, *I pini del Gianicolo*, is a nocturne set near a temple, and provides a mystical atmosphere for what you are about to experience.

At this stage of the pathworking you may find that you are pulled off into the darkness of the forest, or you may continue to walk along the ride. This is where the exercise becomes highly personal and no two people will experience the same sensations. Allow the music to carrying you along and guide your path until the deafening finale …

The final movement, *I pini della Via Appia*, portrays pine trees along the great Appian Way in the misty dawn. Respighi wanted the ground to tremble under the footsteps of his army as the legion advances along the Via Appia in the brilliance of the newly risen sun. If there is an alternative piece of music that suggests the sombreness of pinewoods that you prefer, then feel free to use this during your pathworking. At the end, however, do take a sweet biscuit and hot drink to 'earth' yourself.

Finally, let us reflect on the words of the 19th century American writer, Henry Thoreau, who was one of the first writers to extol the inspirational effects of trees and woods. The following extract relates to the pine trees of New England:

Few come to the woods to see how the pine lives and grows and spires, lifting its evergreen arms to the light, to see its perfect success. Most are content to behold it in the shape of many broad boards brought to market, and deem that its true success. The pine is no more lumber than man is … A pine cut down, a dead pine, is no more a pine than a dead human carcass is a man ... Every creature is better alive than dead, both men ... and pine trees, as life is more beautiful than death.

Chapter Seven

A Magical Celebration of the Wild Hunt

The Wild Hunt is an ancient folk myth known across Europe, Asia and North America featuring a phantom huntsman with horses and hounds, in mad pursuit across the skies or along the ground, or just above it; usually encountered in dark forests during the violent storms of the winter months.

According to the *Encyclopaedia Britannica*, the term 'forest' derived from Latin sources and by the end of the 9th century AD had come to mean a large tract of land including woods, pasture and even whole villages on which the rights of the chase were reserved by the king. The famous old forests of England were areas of this class set aside by the Norman kings, with the legends of Robin Hood and others of his type illustrating the social meaning of the word at that time. Eventually the royal prerogative fell into decay, the legalistic meaning disappeared and 'forest' came to mean wild land covered mainly by trees.

In traditional British Old Craft, the Wild Huntsman is the Lord of Death and the Underworld, and guardian of these forests. His time is from the Autumn to the Spring Equinox when, as the constellation Orion, he dominates the night sky. During this time, he also stands protector for Nature as she slumbers peacefully until the regeneration of spring. These forests have provided the backdrop to much folklore and legend, and violent storms in the forest were once attributed to the furious ride of the Wild Huntsman.

As with many other pre-Christian traditions, however, the widespread belief in the supernatural associations of the Wild Hunt was taken over by the Church and Christianised, with the

Huntsman identified with the Devil or some blasphemous nobleman. Seeing the Wild Hunt was thought to herald some catastrophe such as war or plague, or the death of the one who witnessed it and mortals getting in the path of, or following the Hunt could be kidnapped and brought to the land of the dead. A girl who saw Wild Edric's Ride was warned by her father to put her apron over her head to avoid the sight. Others believed that people's spirits could be pulled away during their sleep to join the cavalcade.

In parts of Britain, the Hunt is said to be that of hell hounds chasing sinners or the unbaptised. In Devon these are known as Yeth or Wisht Hounds; in Cornwall Dando and his Dogs, or the Devil and his Dandy Dogs; in Wales the *Cwn Annwn*, the Hounds of Hell; and in Somerset as Gabriel Hounds or Ratchets. In Devon, the hunt is particularly associated with Wistman's Wood, a rare relict of ancient high-level woodlands of Dartmoor consisting mainly of stunted pedunculate oak trees that grow from between moss-covered boulders and festooned with mosses, lichens and ferns. Its name probably derives from Wishtman's wood, from the dialect word *wisht* meaning 'eerie' or 'uncanny'.

Even historical figures such as St. Guthlac (683–714); Eadric the Wild (an Anglo-Saxon who led English resistance to the Norman Conquest c1068); and Hereward the Wake (died c1070) were reported to have participated in the Wild Hunt. In the *Peterborough Chronicle*, there is an account of the Hunt's appearance at night, beginning with the appointment of a disastrous abbot for the monastery, Henry d'Angely, in 1127:

... many men both saw and heard a great number of huntsmen hunting. The huntsmen were black, huge, and hideous, and rode on black horses and on black he-goats, and their hounds were jet black, with eyes like saucers, and horrible. This was seen in the very deer park of the town of Peterborough, and in all the woods that stretch

*from that same town to Stamford, and in the night the monks heard
them sounding and winding their horns.*

Witnesses were said to have given the number as twenty or thirty
riders, and the phenomena went on for nine weeks, ending at
Easter. An English monk reported a similar cavalcade seen in
Normandy in January 1091. While the earlier sightings of Wild
Hunts were recorded by clerics and portrayed as diabolic, in later
medieval romances, the hunters were seen as coming from the
Faere world; its leaders have also included Gwydion, Gwynn ap
Nudd, King Arthur, King Herla, Woden and Herne the Hunter.
Although often portrayed as an irreverent nobleman who told
God he could keep heaven so long as he could keep on hunting,
the Huntsman is a much older legend, pre-dating Christianity in
Europe.

Many legends are told of his origins, as in that of 'Dando and
his dogs' or 'the dandy dogs': Dando, wanting a drink but having
exhausted what his huntsmen carried, declared he would go to
hell for it and set off with his dogs giving chase. Another legend
recounted how King Herla, having visited the Faere Folk, was
warned not to step down from his horse until the greyhound he
carried jumped down; he found that three centuries had passed
during his visit, and those of his men who dismounted crumbled
to dust. He and his men are still riding, because the greyhound
has yet to jump down.

The story of Herne the Hunter is another that has become part
of contemporary witchcraft, with Herne being identified with
Cernunnos and the Horned God. Although associated with the
Great Park long before kings came to Windsor, according to
legend, Herne was a royal huntsman who saved one of the
Plantagenet king's life by interposing his own body between a
wounded stag and his master. As he lay mortally wounded, a
cunning man appeared out of the forest and told the king that the
only way to save Herne's life was to cut off the stag's antlers and

tie them to the huntsman's head. Herne recovered and enjoyed the king's favour until court politics got in the way and he was dismissed. Herne hanged himself from a great oak that once grew there and has haunted Windsor Great Park ever since, accompanied by baying hounds and riding a black horse, with the ragged antlers still attached to his head.

The object of this phantom hunt varies greatly but the common belief is that it represents the autumn leaves torn from the trees and whirled away by the wintry gales. This extract from another poem, *The Ghost Chase*, by Walter de la Mare paints a more sombre, silent and ghostly view of the Wild Hunt

What sight is this? ... on dazzling snow,
Cold as a shroud beneath the sky,
Swoop into view, the valley through,
Fox, horsemen, hounds — in soundless cry!
Hullà! Hullo! Hulla-hoo!

The voiceless hounds are white as he;
Huntsman and horse — no scarlet theirs;
No fleck, mark, dapple, or spot to see,
White as the North — horses and mares.

They move as in a dream — no stir,
No hoof-fall, music, tongue or steel —
Swift ass a noiseless scimitar
Cutting the snows the winds congeal.

Now they are gone. O dove-white yews!
O sleep-still vale! All silent lies
The calm savanna of the snows,
Beneath the blue of artic skies.
Hullà! Hullo! Hulla-hoo!

It's not surprising that our ancestors saw a phantasmagoria of a Wild Hunt in the swift moving storm clouds scudding across the face of the moon on a winter's night. With the wind howling and trees groaning, the forest sounds outside the cottage or croft would create a visual nightmare of phantom huntsmen, horses and hounds. Added to this, November was traditionally the time when geese were brought nearer the homestead to be fattened for the Midwinter feast, and the mournful call of the wild geese would have echoed over the land. The ghostly Gabriel Hounds, giving the same yelping cry that migrating wild geese make when they pass unseen overhead at night, were taken in the North and West of England as an omen of approaching death. These hounds, with their white bodies and red ears, are found in British, Irish, Welsh and Scottish folklore. The noisy geese, night-flighting in their characteristic V-formations, would keep the superstitious at home in their beds, ensuring that witches would have the woods and forests to themselves.

Although our hunter-gatherer ancestors were an integral part of the ancient woodlands, few traces of prehistoric man are found in what were once densely forested regions. Nevertheless, the spiritual aspects of the pagan hunt are deeply ingrained in our universal subconscious, and a reason why witches must always give the Huntsman respect as the Lord of Death, the Underworld and particularly, as guardian of the forest (Nature).

Many who feel threatened by hunting's history and traditions miss the point that the participants are often closer to the ancestral pagan ideal than those who object to it. This is the Wild Hunt made manifest and the links to the supernatural appearance of grey foxes, spectral deer, ghost packs and horses are never far from the surface of traditional British Old Craft. MFH, Lucy Whaley, recalled the magical poem about hounds running to the grave of their former Master that ends with the words:

Fred whispered to the solemn field,
Bare-headed amongst the mounds,
'Gentlemen, I am taking them Home;
His lordship has called his Hounds.'

She added, 'What hunting has to give each of us depends on what is there already ... I am moved at different times by sidelights of a wider world — as in the bony head of an old horse out at grass, gazing longingly after hounds ...' Another huntsman observed: 'It was almost eerie, the first experience of surviving a screaming hunt like that, of discovering that unbroken link with the Furies, the Maenads, the Wild Hunt and all the other untamed rituals of our ancestors, who knew the meaning of this kind of connection with the wild.'

If the Wild Hunt survives in our collective subconscious, whether we ourselves are hunters or not, then its earthly form (amongst those who *truly* observe the traditions) must surely be the last surviving 'great rite' of our hunter-gatherer forebears.

Sloe Gin — a witch's rescue remedy!

Sloe gin is the countryman's traditional version of 'rescue remedy' that has helped keep the blood flowing during long hours out on the hunting field. Despite its history and importance to general well being, there is no single recipe for this powerful elixir.

Sloes mature in October after the first frost, but this process can be accelerated by putting them in the freezer compartment for a few hours after picking.

Sloe Gin

1 bottle gin
6 oz sloes
4 oz granulated sugar

Pour all the gin from the bottle. Prick the sloes all over with a thick darning needle and put them into the gin bottle. Cover them with the sugar and pour back as much gin as possible. Recap the bottle, turn it upside down to dissolve the sugar and leave to stand. Do this every day for two months; allow the contents to settle for three days and decant into another bottle.

Sloe gin is the witch's recommended toast for the Midwinter festival, and if we are out and about in the woods in the depths of winter, a small hip flask of this warming brew is the perfect libation.

The Path of the Wild Hunt

This pathworking should only be performed out of doors in winter, at the height of a gale, in order to experience the exhilaration of seeing Nature at its wildest. Although we run the risk of being flattened by a falling branch, it is worth courting the danger to sit in the shelter of a large tree and witness the force of the high winds and driving rain. The winter gale can produce the same adrenalin rush as a violent summer storm, and is an ideal energy to draw us into another woodland pathworking.

When you have found a comfortable, sheltered spot, try to focus on the path of the wind by watching the accumulated debris being blown between the trees. The gusts will come in fits and starts, driving leaves and twigs at a furious pace; throwing them into the air and then in a sudden lull, dropping them to the ground. The wind in the overhead branches howls and whistles; sometimes even sounding like the crashing of waves on rocks. There is a wildness here that is both exhilarating and terrifying. Now close your eyes and allow the psycho-drama to build in your mind; visualise yourself being carried along by the wind and see where the journey leads ...

A witch's personal universe does not allow for coincidences and should an image appear — in whatever form — it should be noted and recorded, even if the significance isn't apparent at that precise moment in time. Messages and warnings filter through to us from other planes in all manner of guises and it is up to us to receive and interpret them to the best of our ability. If we chose to ignore them, waiting for something more profound to appear, our 'guardians' may not bother next time!

The Element of Fear

Took the dogs to the woods yesterday and the bluebells are out; the perfume and the rippling blue haze was absolutely gorgeous. I love the woods; they still hold that scary, unpredictable magic feeling. What might be lurking behind the next tree? The movement of the branches causing a flickering dappled sunshine effect. All in the imagination ... until in the silence a pheasant suddenly goes up and you nearly pooh your pants!

When walking alone in the woods even the most seasoned of wood-witches will suddenly be overtaken by the inexplicable sensation that they are being followed. There is the fleeting moment of almost blind terror. We are convinced that there is someone stalking us; the hair on the back of our neck rises; we whirl around to confront the intruder and ... *nothing!* Yet for an incalculable second there *was* the almost tangible sensation of someone being there. We laugh with relief and break the spell ... there is the feeling that the woods themselves are laughing *with* us and the fear disappears.

This sensation is what the Greeks attributed to Panic fear — the sudden, irrational blind terror that strikes without any visible reason or foundation — caused by encountering the Great God Pan in wild and remote places. It is not unusual for a witch to encounter Pan in this way, and we feel that he is still playing games with the unsuspecting, just as he has been doing since the days when he was worshipped in ancient Greece.

Strangely enough, however, there are recognised phobias where some people are genuinely terrified of woods and trees:

Dendrophobia is a morbid fear of trees.

Hylophobia, also known as **Xylophobia** or **Ylophobia**, is a psychological disorder defined by an irrational fear of woods, forests or trees.

Nyctohylophobia is the fear of dark wooded areas or forests at nighttime, from the Greek *nycto-* meaning night; *hylo-* meaning wood, and *-phobia* being an irrational fear.

If you have a sense of foreboding when you consider entering the woods at night you are not an isolated case, and it *is* common among witches to find individuals who find the idea less than desirable. Unfortunately, the present social climate isn't conducive to wandering about the woods alone after dark, and we need to recognize whether our fear is due to social insecurity, or more deep rooted. The woods at night can feel oppressive and full of strange noises: we only have to re-read another chapter 'The Wild Wood' from *The Wind in the Willows*, to experience (by proxy) a frisson of fear evoked by the terror of the Wild Wood.

With the rapid advancement of the consumer age, however, all these links with the ancestors will be completely extinct by the turn of the next century. Traditional country witchcraft will also be consigned to the history books and one wonders whether the Huntsman and his consort, Nature, will wish to inhabit such a soul-less landscape when all the sacred groves have become part of a National Trust's approved nature trail.

As Jennie Gray wrote in *Tales My Mother Never Told Me:*

Where now was the sense of mystery? Where was the sense of reverence, of drama, or poetry? The black impenetrable forest, full of wraiths and shadows, of wild animals and spirits who could tear you limb from limb, or equally show you visions of blinding sublimity, must now be replaced by this small patch of woodland, perhaps ten acres of it altogether, with its threadbare paths and its gap-toothed openness caused by the trampling of too many feet.

With all this in mind, *Traditional Witchcraft for Woods and Forests* does not reflect the modern 'theme park' attitude to the woodlands. Nature quickly revolts when humans tamper with the established order of things but, given a chance, she very soon readjusts herself. She creates her own balance and needs to remain in the hands of those guardians of the forest who love and understand her. Hopefully, this book will encourage a new generation of witches to have the courage to follow the age-old observances (in spirit if not in practice) and help return power to the *genius loci* of the forest.

Sources & Bibliography

Collected Rhymes and Verses, Walter de la Mare (Faber & Faber)

Country Seasons, Philip Clucas (Windward)

The Country-side Cook Book, Gail Duff (Prism Press)

The Covenant of the Wild, Stephen Budiansky (Phoenix)

Encyclopaedia of the British Countryside (Drive Publications)

The Ever-changing Woodland, ed Euan Dunn (Readers Digest)

The Heritage Trees of Britain & Northern Ireland, Jon Stokes and Donald Rodger (Constable)

The Lore of the Forest, Alexander Porteous (Senate)

Nature's Changing Seasons, Peter a Gerrard (Sphere)

Nature Through the Seasons, Richard Adams and Max Hooper (Penguin)

Root & Branch: British Magical Tree Lore, Mélusine Draco and Paul Harriss (ignotus)

The Tree Book, J Edward Milner (Collins & Brown)

Trees of Britain & Northern Europe, David More and John White (Cassell)

Trees in the Wild, Gerald Wilkinson (BCA)

A Witch's Treasury of the Countryside, Mélusine Draco and Paul Harriss (ignotus)

MOON
BOOKS

Moon Books invites you to begin or deepen your
encounter with Paganism, in all its rich, creative,
flourishing forms.